Think Green, Take Action

Other Recently Published Teacher Ideas Press Titles

Story Starters and Science Notebooking: Developing Student Thinking Through Literacy and Inquiry
Sandy Buczynski and Kristin Fontichiaro

Fun with Finance: Math + Literacy = Success
Written and Illustrated by Carol Peterson

Paper Action Figures of the Imagination: Clip, Color, and Create
Paula Montgomery

Fairy Tales Readers Theatre
Anthony D. Fredericks

Shakespeare Kids: Performing His Plays, Speaking His Words
Carole Cox

Family Matters: Adoption and Foster Care in Children's Literature
Ruth Lyn Meese

Solving Word Problems for Life, Grades 6–8
Melony A. Brown

Abraham Lincoln and His Era: Using the American Memory Project to Teach with Primary Sources
Bobbi Ireland

Brushing Up on Grammar: An Acts of Teaching Approach
Joyce Armstrong Carroll, EdD, HLD, and Edward E. Wilson

The Comic Book Curriculum: Using Comics to Enhance Learning and Life
James Rourke

Hello Hi-Lo: Readers Theatre Math
Jeff Sanders and Nancy I. Sanders

War Stories for Readers Theatre: World War II
Suzanne I. Barchers

Think Green, Take Action

Books and Activities for Kids

Daniel A. Kriesberg

Illustrated by Kathleen A. Price

A Teacher Ideas Press Book

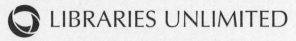
LIBRARIES UNLIMITED

AN IMPRINT OF ABC-CLIO, LLC
Santa Barbara, California • Denver, Colorado • Oxford, England

Library of Congress Cataloging-in-Publication Data

Kriesberg, Daniel A.
   Think green, take action : books and activities for kids / Daniel A. Kriesberg;
illustrated by Kathleen A. Price.
       p. cm.
   "A Teacher Ideas Press Book".
   Includes bibliographical references and index.
    ISBN 978-1-59884-378-1 (hard copy : alk. paper)—ISBN 978-1-59884-379-8
(e-book) 1. Environmental education—Activity programs. 2. Environmental
sciences—Study and teaching (Elementary) 3. Environmental sciences—Study
and teaching (Elementary)—Activity programs. 4. Environmental
sciences—Juvenile literature—Bibliography. I. Price, Kathleen A. ill. II. Title.
    GE70.K76 2010
    333.72—dc22   2010014409

ISBN: 978-1-59884-378-1
EISBN: 978-1-59884-379-8

14   13   12   11   10   1   2   3   4   5

This book is also available on the World Wide Web as an eBook.
Visit http://www.abc-clio.com for details.

Libraries Unlimited
An Imprint of ABC-CLIO, LLC

ABC-CLIO, LLC
130 Cremona Drive, P.O. Box 1911
Santa Barbara, California 93116-1911

This book is printed on acid-free paper ∞

Manufactured in the United States of America

To Zack and Scott, for the sake of my grandchildren and great grandchildren, I hope your generation does a better job then mine as stewards of the earth.

Contents

Acknowledgments

I'd like to give special thanks to the librarians at the Bayville Free Library and Janet Reeves at the Kumar Wang Library for all their help in finding the books I needed for this project. I'd like to thank Sharon Coatney for all her help and guidance throughout the writing of this book; she patiently answered all my questions. Of course, my wife deserves a lot of credit for her patience and support throughout the writing of this book. Perhaps most important of all are my students over the years, who helped develop the activities in this book.

CHAPTER 1

Why and How to Teach Green

Combining the power of story and hands-on learning, the recommended books in this volume give students the knowledge and skills they need to understand environmental problems and take steps to help solve them.

Whether we want to admit it or not, human activity is affecting the health of the planet. Humans have not truly considered the impact we are having on the environment as we go about our daily lives. We have not paid the true costs of using the water, air, and land the way we do.

Damage has been done and the cumulative effect of our actions is building to the point where unless things change, the damage will be great and the problems will not be solved. However, there is hope, and the hope does not come from a miracle invention. There is hope because the solutions come from the same place as the problems, our actions. Humans have caused the problems and humans can solve the problems. The increase in environmental awareness and the changes in lifestyle that have occurred demonstrate that there is a desire to make a difference and improve the environment. Adults are only starting the process; the future depends on young people.

Young people today want to make a difference but they need the skills and knowledge to be effective agents of change. Switching from an incandescent lightbulb to a compact fluorescent lightbulb is a step in the right direction, but is it going to offset the impact humans are having on the planet? To make a long-lasting and effective change instead of a simple gesture, more must be done.

Students need knowledge in order to make changes. This begins with understanding the basics of ecology and the processes scientists use to gain information.

This knowledge will help them to understand environmental problems and issues. Students need not simply depend on "experts" to tell them what to do. They can learn how to learn so that they can make informed choices. As new issues arise, students will be able to learn about them, think critically about them, and make good choices. Only as informed citizens can students take effective action to help solve environmental problems.

Students go through a process as they learn to become environmental stewards. The three stages are:

Stage One: Empathy and Connections

Stage Two: Understanding

Stage Three: Action

The first step is simply making the connections that foster a relationship with the natural world through love and empathy. From this point, students will be motivated to understand ecological inter-relationships and environmental issues because they will care about what is happening. With caring and understanding, students are then able to move on to stage three, where they have the desire and ability to help solve environmental problems and from there can take action.

In general, the focus for younger children ages 6 through 10 should be on the activities and books that foster empathy for and connections to the natural world. Stage two books and activities are geared more toward middle grade students, 10–13 years, old enough to begin understanding environmental issues. The third stage is best for older students ages 13 and up. At this age, they can apply what they have learned. Students can become involved in efforts to help the environment. If older students have not experienced stages one and two in some manner, teaching them stage three will be less effective. Some younger students may be ready for the next stage depending on their experiences. Teach what makes sense for the age and experience of the students. This is not a completely linear process; there will be times to combine and integrate activities and books from more than one stage.

For thousands of years, children have learned by listening to stories from their elders. The stories were the way that knowledge was passed down from generation to generation. These stories held the lessons that taught children how to behave, what to do, and how to live. Today, we may not be spellbinding storytellers, and there is much more competition for a child's attention, but the stories in the books discussed in this volume still resonate more effectively than speeches and lectures to convey inspiration, hope, motivation, and knowledge. Even among older students, these books are a great way to set the tone for a lesson and grab their attention. It is much better to simply start reading and draw the students in with words and pictures instead of the constant mantra, "OK, be quiet now, everyone listen."

Whether you read the entire book to the class or just part of the picture book, whether it is non-fiction or a chapter book or a picture book, you are telling a story that has many gifts. The books serve as models of truly wonderful writing and illustrations. The students learn effective writing styles, different writing genres, and new ways to present information. From all the books, students learn about issues in an entertaining and informative way. The illustrations speak a different language and touch students in magical ways.

Since the books are such a key component of getting the most out of these activities, your school and local libraries are going to very helpful. They will be able to obtain the books you need and even have suggestions about new ideas not covered in this book. Working with your librarians can give students more opportunities to hear or read the books. This book can integrate the library with other curriculum areas. It will help the students to see the library as a place to learn about current events and taking action to help the world around them. The library will also be the place to go for research. Some of the activities will depend on the students gathering information. The library will be where they can find what they need, not just from the Internet, but also from books, magazines, and other forms of media. Only by using the library for themselves will students learn the skills they need to do their own research and become lifetime learners. The resources in the library will be the tools they use to learn and make a difference.

As students read the books or as the books are read to them, there are a number of ways they can respond. You can have them write reviews, book-jacket quotes, their own personal versions, lists of questions, add their own illustrations, or of course they can simply read and enjoy. The lessons in this book are primarily based on a hands-on approach to learning. Students learn best by doing. It is better to design and conduct an experiment yourself rather than to simply read about doing experiments. It is better to interview an environmental hero than to just read about someone in a textbook. It is better to sample the insect population to determine the health of the ecosystem than read about it on a Web site. When students are active and discovering on their own, they are learning more than just the content—they are also gaining the skills that they need to be lifelong learners. And the lessons are interesting and fun!

The best way to teach about the environment is to be out in the environment, so many of the lessons in this book are set outdoors. One important idea to remember when deciding whether it is worth the extra effort to take students into the schoolyard or a nearby park is that there is a difference between teaching and learning. Just because we teach something does not mean that students are going to learn it. Teaching about erosion, even with an exciting YouTube video of a mudslide, is not the same or as effective as seeing erosion in action. When students see something for themselves, they know it is real; when they see it in their own lives, they become connected to the concept.

Teachers can use the outdoors as a classroom, and a schoolyard is a perfect place to begin. Students do not need a national park; they just need some open space. They are able to find the wonder and knowledge anywhere outdoors if given the opportunity. The outdoor lessons in this book can be done in virtually any schoolyard.

There are going to be some distractions when taking students outdoors. However, they must understand that the outdoors is just an extension of the classroom; it is not a place to goof around. Just as in the classroom, consistent discipline will make all the difference. If needed, you may have to bring the class back inside to make the point that you expect their cooperation.

The extra time that it takes to walk outdoors is well worth the experiences gained being in direct contact with the subject matter. Even if it is not possible to take students outside, there are opportunities to bring natural materials into the classroom. It is these direct experiences that create the empathy with the natural world needed to make the connections and experience love for the environment.

Whenever possible, adapt these activities to your local community. Before students can understand what is happening in faraway places, they need to know what is happening where they live. With this understanding, they can apply what they learn to more abstract situations. When local issues are used, students can be directly involved in learning about the environmental problem and helping to solve it. By focusing on a local issue instead of someplace far away, students can work directly with those involved in the issue.

Optimism makes a difference; students are not going to work to solve problems if they do not believe their actions matter—they will lose hope. That is why showing them there is hope and that problems can be solved is so important. It is vital for students to hear about success stories. So much of the news on environmental issues is focused on the negative. Students hear more about the animals that are going extinct than the animals that have been protected. They need to learn how the water quality in many rivers has improved, how trees have regrown after deforestation in the Northeast, how millions of acres of land has been set aside for protection, and many more stories. These success stories are examples of how the knowledge and skills that students are learning will make a difference.

Teaching students about heroes is another great opportunity to share success stories. We all need to know that there are people who have made a difference and who are making a difference right now. When children learn the stories of environmental heroes, they are learning about environmental issues, they are learning how people take on challenges, and, most importantly, they are learning that what a person does matters.

It is also important to teach without using fear. Fear may grab some attention in the beginning, but is not a very good motivator in the long run. Fear takes away hope. It does not lead to a long-term change. What is appropriate for a 16-year-old is not the same as for a 7-year-old. When teaching students about World War II, we gear the lessons to the age of the students. If too much emphasis is placed on teaching young children about environmental problems at an early age, they will grow disconnected and feel powerless to change anything. They will suffer from what author David Sobel calls "ecophobia," a fear and disconnect from the environment. This can happen to older students and adults as well if facing the facts is not balanced by stories of hope and success. Teaching environmental issues in the classroom is not a simple task. There are real problems and real concerns. Many of the issues are full of gray areas, they are not always black and white, and the problems are not easy to fix. There is still much for scientists to figure out about the causes of the problems and the effects they have on the health of our planet. As students learn about these issues, they need to understand that solutions will take creative thinking. There are often two or even more sides of any given issue, and depending on the point of view, there can be very different ideas about how to solve a problem or even disagreement that there is a problem.

As teachers, we need to show students various points of view when they are based on honest scientific disagreement. To do this, we need to keep in mind how science works. The key is to understand the difference between a fact and a theory. A fact is an observation that is made on a repeated basis. A theory is an explanation of events based on facts. A theory is not a guess, and it is not based on opinions—it is based on the available facts. As more facts are gathered, theories may gain support, or scientists may come to the conclusion they were wrong and adjust the theory. Over time and as more facts are known, scientists will reach an understanding and general consensus. When learning about an environmental problem, students need to look at where information is coming from and ask themselves if there is a bias. There are instances when science is clouded by political agendas.

Just because theories change, scientists are sometimes wrong, and there are varying points of view, the process of science should not be used as a call for inaction. We need to make decisions about protecting the environment with the knowledge we have. More knowledge will only help us to make better decisions.

One of the major problems facing teachers today is how to find time to teach everything they are supposed to teach. Material is always being added to the curriculum and very rarely is anything ever taken out. The lessons in this book are not just geared toward being taught in science class. Depending on your curriculum and subject, there are lessons that can be used in social studies, math, science, language arts, and the arts. As you read though the ideas in this book, try to see opportunities to integrate the lessons into various subject areas. If environmental issues are integrated throughout the curriculum, students realize how the skills they are learning in one subject apply to a real-world situation. Learning about environmental issues doesn't have to be a whole new unit to teach; it can be part of the work you are already doing.

The activities in this book will also help teachers meet learning standards for the American Association of School Librarians, the American Association for the Advancement of Science, the National Council for the Social Studies, the National Council of Teachers of English, and the International Reading Association. Many of the state standards in these core curriculum areas can be met by using the activities in this book. Using these activities to meet the standards will not only help students, but will also help teachers gain support from parents and administrators for this kind of teaching.

The organization of the book follows the three stages of becoming environment stewards mentioned earlier. The books and activities in chapter 2 support your efforts to create empathy and connection. In chapters 3, 4, 5, the activities and books help students understand the major environmental issues facing the world. Chapter 6 focuses on activities and books that teach how to help solve these problems. Each chapter in this book has two parts. Part one is a bibliography of books that address the topic of the chapter. There is a summary of the books and some ideas for using each one. Part two of each chapter focuses on an environmental issue by providing activities to help students understand it. No one is going to do all the activities in the book, but just as taking some action is better than taking no action, doing some of the activities is better than doing none of them.

References

Diamond, Jared. *Collapse: How Societies Choose or Fail to Succeed.* New York: Penguin Books, 2005. 0-14-303655-6.

Hutchinson, David. *Growing Up Green: Education for Ecological Renewal.* New York: Teachers College Press, 1998. 0-8077-3724-0.

Louv, Richard. *Last Child in the Woods: Saving Our Children from Nature-Deficit Disorder.* Chapel Hill, NC: Algonquin Books, 2005. 978-1-56512-391-5.

Sobel, David. *Beyond Ecophobia.* Great Barrington, MA: Orion Society, 1996. 0-913098-50-7.

Organizations

Publications from these organizations will help to connect the activities and books to academic standards in science, library studies, language arts, and social studies. They can be used to help demonstrate the importance of these lessons and gain support for teaching these topics.

The American Association for the Advancement of Science
1200 New York Avenue NW
Washington, DC 20005
202-326-6400
http://www.project2061.org/publications/bsl/online/index.php

American Association of School Librarians (AASL)
American Library Association
50 East Huron Street
Chicago, IL 60611-2795
http://www.ala.org/aasl

International Reading Association
800 Barksdale Road
P.O. Box 8139
Newark, DE 19714-8139
http://www.reading.org/downloads/resources/545standards2003/index.html

National Council for the Social Studies
8555 Sixteenth Street, Suite 500
Silver Spring, MD 20910
301-588-1800
http://www.socialstudies.org/standards/curriculum

The National Council of Teachers of English
1111 W. Kenyon Road, Urbana, IL 61801-1096
217-328-3870 or 877-369-6283
http://www.ncte.org/standards

CHAPTER 2

Understanding the Ecology of Your Home Place

Books

Aruego, Jose, and Ariane Dewey. *Weird Friends: Unlikely Allies in the Animal Kingdom.* San Diego, CA: Gulliver Books, 2006. 0-15-202128-0.

Bright, colorful, entertaining illustrations effectively help to explain the ecological concept of mutualism. Students will be amazed at the way these animals have adapted to help each other. This book uses examples from both aquatic and terrestrial habitats. The interrelationships show students how interconnected life is on Earth. With a little research, students will be able to find mutualism and other forms of symbiosis in their local ecosystems.

Bang, Molly, and Penny Chisholm. *Living Sunlight: How Plants Bring the Earth to Life.* New York: Blue Sky Press, Scholastic, 2009. 978-0-545-04422-6.

This book does a great job of showing the wonder of photosynthesis and its importance in maintaining life on Earth. In simple terms, Molly Bang and Penny Chisholm use words and detailed paintings

to explain how plants take carbon dioxide and water and change it to the oxygen and sugars upon which animals depend. The back of the book has additional information and explains the symbolism behind the illustrations.

Brenner, Barbara. *One Small Place by the Sea.* Illustrated by Tom Leonard. New York: HarperCollins, 2004. 0688171834.

Brenner, Barbara. *One Small Place in a Tree.* Illustrated by Tom Leonard. New York: HarperCollins, 2004. 068817180X.

These books will help students focus on one spot and make observations about the interrelationships and changes that take place over time. *One Small Place by the Sea* focuses on the happenings in a tide pool. In *One Small Place in a Tree*, the action begins when a bear uses a tree for a scratching post. This sets off an interesting set of interrelationships. The realistic illustrations add a strong visual impact. These are good books to read as the students make observations in their secret spots.

Brown, Ruth. *The World That Jack Built.* New York: Dutton, 1991. 0525446354.

This book is based on the rhyme, "The House that Jack Built." Ruth Brown shows the connections between the construction of Jack's house and the surrounding landscape. As Jack builds more and more, the surrounding land changes. Dramatic illustrations portray this transition.

Brown, Ruth. *The Big Sneeze.* New York: Random House, 1993. 009942150X

When a farmer's sneeze blows a fly into a spiderweb, it sets off a chain reaction. This is a humorous description of how a simple act can lead from one thing to another. It is a fun way to introduce the concept of interrelationships.

Crenson, Victoria. *Horseshoe Crabs and Shorebirds: The Story of a Food Web.* Illustrated by Annie Cannon. Tarrytown, NY: Marshall Cavendish, 2003. 0-7614-5115-3.

This story of the relationship between horseshoe crabs and migrating shorebirds is a great example of why we need to understand the interrelationships that are part of the natural world. Every spring, millions of horseshoe crabs lay billions of eggs along the shores of the North Atlantic. At the same time, huge flocks of shorebirds and gulls are migrating north. This migration requires a great deal of energy. Only by feeding on the eggs will the shorebirds have enough energy to make it to their breeding grounds. With the decline in the horseshoe crab population, the shorebirds are now threatened. It is all connected.

Fisher, Aileen. *The Story Goes On.* Illustrated by Mique Moriuchi. Brookfield, CT: Roaring Brook Press, 2002. 1-59643-037-0.

This is a simple story showing the connections in a food chain. Beginning with a seed that is eaten by an insect that is eaten by a frog, which is eaten by a snake that is eaten by a hawk, the story takes an interesting turn when a man with a shotgun kills the hawk. This can prompt a discussion of the role humans play in a food cycle. The paintings are brightly colored and some are done over newsprint, which gives the book a childlike wonder.

Godkin, Celia. *Wolf Island.* Markham, ON: Fitzhenry & Whiteside, 1993. 978-1554550074.

When a pack of wolves leaves its island home, dramatic changes take place. With no wolves, the deer population rises. With more deer, there is eventually less food for the deer and other herbivores, so they starve. With fewer herbivores, the predators do not have enough food, so they also starve. It is not until the wolves return that the dynamic balance of the island is restored.

Goodman, Susan E. *Stems, Stamens, and Seeds: How Plants Fit in the World.* Photographs by Michael Doolittle. Brookfield, CT: Millbrook Press, 2001. 0-7613-1874-7.

Sometimes plants are overlooked while teaching students about the natural world. However, plants have amazing and interesting adaptations and are easier to observe then most animals. This book explains the adaptations plants have made to fit in their habitat, obtain sunlight, protect themselves, and reproduce. Your students will pay more attention to plants and better understand the concept of adaptations after reading this book.

Goodman, Susan, E. *Claws, Coats, and Camouflage: The Way Animals Fit into the World.* Photographs by Michael Doolittle. Brookfield, CT: Millbrook Press, 2001. 0-0-7613-1865-8.

A companion to *Stems, Stamens, and Seeds,* this book has great examples of the many wondrous ways that animals have adapted to survive in their habitats. The text and photographs show the reader examples of how animals are adapted to certain habitats, where they are able to protect themselves, obtain food, and reproduce. The book ends with the reminder that humans are animals as well and we have our own adaptations to survive.

Himmelman, John. *A Dandelion's Life.* New York: Children's Press, 1998. 0-516-21177-3.

A simple nonfiction picture book about the life cycle of a dandelion inspires one to pay attention to the natural world, even the weeds that grow on our lawns. The illustrations will motivate students to look closely at dandelions and other common lawn plants as they follow the changes through the seasons. This is a good introduction to seeing the wonder in the everyday.

Jenkins, Steve, and Robin Page. *What Do You Do with a Tail Like This?* Boston: Houghton Mifflin Company, 2003. 0-618-25628-8.

This Caldecott Honor Book is a great way to teach students about animal adaptations. There are examples of many different ways that animals use their tails, ears, noses, eyes, and other body parts to survive. Animals have adaptations to fit the habitats they live in. If the habitat is destroyed, they cannot just move somewhere else.

Jenkins, Steve, and Robin Page. *How Many Ways Can You Catch a Fly?* Boston: Houghton Mifflin Company, 2008. 978-0-618-96634-9.

Written and illustrated by the same authors as *What Do You Do With a Tail Like This?*, their latest book is a great way to show students the wide diversity of adaptations animals have to survive. There are examples from all over the world of how animals find food, shelter, and reproduce. Students will see the true wonder of animal adaptations.

Kramer, Stephen. *How to Think Like a Scientist: Answering Questions by the Scientific Method.* Illustrated by Felicia Bond. New York: HarperCollins, 1987. 0690045654.

This book is a good introduction for students learning the scientific method. Just as science begins with a question, so does this book. From this beginning, the author shows each step of the scientific method. By using cartoon-like drawings and everyday situations, the author and illustrator show readers how the scientific method relates to a young person's life. This book will help students understand the nature of science.

LaMarche, Jim. *The Raft.* New York: HarperCollins, 2000. 0-688-13977-9.

A boy named Nicky must spend the summer at his grandmother's house in the country. He is not happy about the situation. However, when he discovers an old raft on the river's edge, a new world opens up. He explores the river with his grandmother and begins watching and drawing wildlife. He begins to see the wonder and mystery of the river and becomes a river rat just like his grandmother.

Lehn, Barbara. *What Is a Scientist?* Brookfield, CT: Millbrook Press, 1999. 0761312986.

Using photographs and straightforward text, this book will help teachers introduce and reinforce the scientific method. It begins by defining a scientist as someone who asks questions and then tries to find the answers. The book shows the different ways scientists find answers and acknowledges that they are not always successful. This is a good stepping-stone for asking the questions we need answered to protect the environment.

London, Jonathon. *Giving Thanks.* Illustrated by Gregory Manchess. Cambridge, MA: Candlewick Press, 2003. 0-7636-1680-X.

While walking with his father, a boy learns how to show gratitude to the plants and animals, sky and wind and all else that they see, feel, and hear. The text along with the paintings makes this a good book for showing students a way to appreciate the wonder and gifts of the natural world.

Martin, Bill, Jr., and Michael Sampson. *I Love Our Earth.* Photographs by Dan Lipou. Watertown, MA: Charlesbridge Press, 2006. 978-1-58089-106-6.

The words and photographs in this book celebrate the wonderful diversity of people and places. This is a good book to read aloud as an introduction to lessons on seeing the wonder in the natural world and as a reminder that people are part of what is going on.

Morrison, Gordon. *Nature in the Neighborhood.* Boston: Houghton Mifflin Books, 2004. 0-547-01548-8.

This wonderful book helps students realize there are a lot of interesting animals and plants living in any neighborhood. The main text tells the story of robins, toads, squirrels, crabgrass, and other urban plants and animals. The bottom of each page has notes with even more information. The illustrations will help students indentify the plants in their own neighborhoods.

Post, Hans, and Irene Geode. *Creepy Crawlies.* Asheville, NC: Front Street. 2005. 1932425659.

This book combines the story of a cat named Lika with amazing facts and information about the small insects and other invertebrates that live in our homes and backyards. The reader follows Lika's adventures as she wanders around inside and outside her home finding all sorts of amazing animals.

Sayre, April Pulley. *Trout Are Made of Trees.* Illustrated by Kate Endle. Watertown, MA: Charlesbridge Publishing, 2008. 978-1-58089-137-0.

In simple text and bright illustrations, this book demonstrates the connections in a food chain from a leaf through a fish and back to leaves again. What makes this book interesting is how it shows that food chains link one habitat to another. Animals truly are what they eat, and that includes us.

Toft, Kim Michelle. *The World We Want.* Watertown, MA: Charlesbridge Publishing, 2005. 1580891144.

While students understand the interconnections within an ecosystem, this book will help them see how ecosystems around the world are connected. By traveling from a rainforest to a coral reef, students will better understand that places are connected to each other through plant and animal life. When something happens in one place, it can affect what is going on in another, even if it is far away. The bold, bright illustrations give the reader an expanding view of the world's ecosystems as more and more are included. The last pages of the book provide additional background information on the animals and plants of each ecosystem.

Activities

Before one can understand and solve environmental problems, one must have a connection to and knowledge of the land. For all of us, this means having a basic knowledge of ecology and a sense of place. The more we understand about how something works, the better able we are to solve problems. The more we see the wonder, have fun, and feel part of the stories of the land, the more we will care about the land. The same is true for children. If we want kids to become aware of environmental issues and take action to help ease the impact humans are having on the environment, they must first build an understanding and a love for the place in which they live. Without caring, there is no action; without knowledge, there is no effective action. This connection begins with awareness that is borne from becoming a better observer. We all need to be more aware of our surroundings in order to notice the changes. These activities are a way to begin developing the connection and understanding needed to solve environmental problems.

Secret Spot

In order to build awareness, connections, and knowledge, there is no better tool than a secret spot. A secret spot is a place a student selects near his or her home that he or she can return to on a repeated basis. It is spot where the child can simply sit and observe the natural world. A secret spot can be in a backyard, side yard, front yard, park, or nearby nature preserve. The key is that the secret spot is located where the child can safely and easily go to sit on a regular basis.

The time spent in a secret spot teaches a child that being attentive is rewarded with wonder and knowledge. The wonder comes from observing life, whether it is a drop of water rainbowing on a leaf edge or a sow bug crawling on a rotten log. It is seeing a mockingbird build a nest in a nearby bush or listening to a rustle in the leaves and wondering who goes there. The knowledge comes from learning for oneself by direct observation. In a secret spot, children learn about the natural world for themselves. They are not dependent on a book or Web site. All of this comes by having senses made for wonder.

Materials: none

Procedure:
To teach your students about secret spots, start by finding and using a secret spot on the school grounds. This is where you go as a group to teach your students the power of a secret spot. It does not have to be in a forest, by a pond, or on the beach. It just needs to be outside, even on a lawn or next to a single tree.

Have students begin each session in the secret spot with silence. They should sit or stand in silence and focus on what their senses reveal. This starts by paying attention to the surrounding area just a few feet away. The students should observe all around, asking themselves what can I see, hear, feel, and smell? With my students, I suggest staying away from taste. Encourage them to go from the close-up and move their senses out to about ten feet. Again, what can you see, hear, feel, and smell? Next, the students take their senses further outward as far as they can. As your students use their secret spots more, they are better able to spend more time in silence. The longer and more intently they observe, the more wonder and knowledge they will gain.

Students can do the following activities at their secret spot or anywhere else that helps to create a sense of place and knowledge of ecology.

Sketching

Sketching is a great way to become more observant and does not always have to be about creating a realistic drawing. Nature journal sketching has a different goal. The goal of nature journal sketching is to increase awareness and make observations. For students who have difficulty expressing their observations in writing, sketching is another avenue for recording. If more is observed by creating the sketch, then it is a good sketch. If the sketch helps one to remember more, then it is a good sketch. The sketch is not judged by the realism of the work. Nature journal sketching means seeing each object that is drawn as a unique subject. It means seeing the actual details instead of drawing the object that we see in our mind's eye. It means that the student does not draw a tree that has a hole for an owl or a tree that looks like a lollipop unless that is how the tree really looks. They should not draw a worm with eyes. Ask them: Is the water really blue? Is the tree trunk really brown?

Materials: journals, pencils

Procedure:

Blind Contour Drawing
A great way for students to learn to sketch for observation is blind contour drawing. This technique forces students to look at the unique qualities of what they are drawing. Students should pick a small object such as a leaf, twig, flower, or shell. They are going to sketch the object without looking at the paper and by looking only at the object. It works best by having them imagine an ant crawling along the edge of the object. As they follow the ant's journey around the edge, they draw the outline on the paper without ever taking their eyes off the ant. The sketch needs to only take a minute or two. Have them label that sketch number 1. Now they repeat the sketch and label it number 2. Before anyone can ask "Is this a good drawing?", ask "Did you observe something new the second time you sketched the object that you did not notice before?" If they answer yes, then it is a good sketch. They can do another sketch to learn more about the object.

Memory Drawing: Memory drawings are another technique that helps students become better observers. It is the opposite of blind contour drawing. Here students study the object for a minute or so without drawing. They need to truly focus and study the object to see what makes it unique. Then they put the object down and sketch a picture without looking at the object. To judge whether it is a good drawing, have them make two or more sketches. If the students noticed something they did not observe before, then it is a good drawing.

Gesture Drawing: Gesture drawings are quick sketches that focus on the general shape of an object. This technique is good for observing larger objects such as trees or entire landscapes. Students sketch by capturing the basic shapes in quick, fluid lines.

Free Sketching: In free sketching, students draw any way they please. It might be a combination of the above techniques, or the students simply draw. The emphasis is on observation and not the artistic quality of the drawings.

From *Think Green, Take Action: Books and Activities for kids* by Daniel A. Kriesberg. Santa Barbara, CA: Libraries Unlimited. Copyright © 2010.

Nature Journals

Journals are another important tool of observation and learning. They can be used in conjunction with a secret spot or on their own. The goal of nature journal writing is to be more attentive and to create a record of observations. Journals have many purposes; however, the goal here is to help make students more aware of their surroundings. The focus is on the observations and not on the quality of the writing.

Materials: journals, pens or pencils

Procedure:
Begin by taking students outdoors to explain the format of journal entries. The first step is for everyone to stand or sit in silence using the secret spot opening routine. The students should pick something to focus on and observe it carefully. After five minutes or so, they write a four-part journal entry:

1. Heading: On the top of the page, students write the date, location, time, and a couple of words about the weather. Each of these details is important information that adds to the observations.

2. The second step is for the students to record their observations. They should write at least seven observations. The student should be attentive to nonhuman nature. It is not the place for recording emotions, likes, and dislikes or reactions; it is a time to simply record what was observed. Students should not write something like "The snow was lovely" or "The birds sang cheerfully." They should write what they saw, heard, smelled, and felt. Students should not write comments such as "The sun feels good and reminds me of my birthday" or "The tree is big." Instead of one observation about several items, it is better to make many detailed observations about one item.

3. Another part of the entry is the question. At the end of each entry, students should ask a question about what they observed. With my students, I answer the questions if I can, look it up if I need to, and often simply write "good question." Often I will not be able to answer the question and can only marvel and wonder. Sometimes it will be a question the students can answer themselves through their own inquiry either by doing some research or by simply continuing to make observations over time. This is a great opportunity for students to learn for themselves by being their own experts.

4. The final part of the journal entry is a sketch. The students make at least one sketch using blind contour, memory, gesture, or free sketch, and should label their sketches.

Remember, the goal of the nature entries is not poetic writing or critical-thinking essays. The goal of the drawing is not an artistic masterpiece. The goal of the writing and sketching is to raise awareness, increase the powers of observation, and inspire wonder.

Maps

Maps are another great way to record observations in a visual format. Each map begins on a sheet of paper by putting an X to mark where the student is sitting in the secret spot. Then they can make one or more of the following maps.

Materials: journals

Procedure:

Sound Map: While sitting in their secret spot, students listen carefully and mark on a map what they heard and where they heard the sound. They can make sound maps on more than one visit to add new sounds and mark the ones they heard again.

Animal and Plant Map: Students make a map of the different plants growing around their secret spot. They also record the animals they see and the animals' signs.

Wonder Map: Students draw a map highlighting the landmarks, interesting things that have happened, questions they have, and anything else that strikes their fancy.

The Ultimate Nature Entry

A culminating activity for the secret spot is the Ultimate Nature Entry Project. It is designed to have students conduct an in-depth study of one part of their secret spot or the schoolyard. The project integrates a variety of skills into a study of their place. The Ultimate Nature Entry Project is a way to truly get students engaged with their secret spot. There are a number of activities they will undertake to become more engaged in their secret spot. It is a good idea to model as much of the activities as you can by setting up a project area on the school grounds. The project is done within a two-meter by two-meter square in which they will make a long-term study. Each child will become an expert on his or her square.

Materials: journals, poster board, art materials

Procedure:

Here is a list of possible activities the students can do in their square. You may pick and choose as many as you think your students can do.

1. Describe the location of your square.

2. Dig a hole in the soil. Describe the soil.

3. Make a list of all the animals you see in your square over the next few weeks. (You do not need the exact name, you can make up a name and describe the animal.) What is the population of each animal?

4. Make a list of the plants in your square over the next few weeks. (You do not need the exact name, you can make up a name that describes the plant.) What is the estimated population of each plant?

5. Take at least six photographs of life in the square over the next few weeks.

6. Complete five nature entries.

7. Draw a map of the square.

8. Make an art project using the square as a source of inspiration and/or materials.

9. Pick an animal or plant that is living in your square and list at least 20 facts you observe and 20 other facts from a book, Web site, or other source.

10. Write a report at least three paragraphs long about the animal or plant you picked. The report should include your observations and the facts you researched. Be sure to cite the source of information. Attach a handwritten or typed copy in your journal.

11. What interrelationships do you observe?

12. What evidence of food chains do you observe?

13. Are there any examples of symbiosis in your area?

14. Describe any fungus in your square.

15. What did you think of this project?

16. Parent signature on the bottom of sheet.

17. Hand in this sheet with the project.

Thinking Like a Scientist

To solve environmental problems, we need to understand how science works. Science is what helps us recognize and then solve the problems. Understanding science begins with understanding how scientists learn about the world. These activities model the scientific process of gathering facts and developing theories. Students need to understand that a theory is not a guess. It is the best explanation of the facts that are gathered. Later, if more facts are gathered, they may reveal a different theory that better explains the observations or confirms the current theory. Changing a theory is part of the process of science. By basing science on facts, it provides us with the information to understand the natural world and make better decisions regarding our impact. It is only with this information that we can find solutions that will work. These activities model how scientists gather information, and as new information becomes available, a theory is confirmed or refined or even rejected. They also demonstrate how scientists learn about things they cannot see.

String Tubes

Materials: Empty toilet paper roll (or some other cylinder you can poke holes through). Two shoelaces. Poke two holes on each side of the tube. Thread the shoelaces through the holes, making an X inside the tube.

Procedure:

Hold the tube up and ask the students to draw what they think it looks like inside the tube. Have some of the students share their ideas.

Hold up the tube again and pull on the shoelaces one at a time, but do not pull them all the way out. After observing the way the strings move, have the students make a second drawing of what they think the shoelaces look like inside. Have some of the students share their ideas.

Test the ideas by having the students predict which lace will move when lace A is pulled.

Discuss how this activity mirrors the process scientists go through to learn about the world. First, they gather facts from what they observe on a repeated basis. Next, they put the facts together to develop a theory that explains what is being observed. Be sure to emphasize that scientists base their explanations on facts. You can repeat the activity by making other designs in the tube, for example, twisting the strings together.

Mystery Boxes

Materials: shoebox, small object

Procedure:

Place an object in the box and tape the top down.

Hold the box up and ask the students what facts they can observe about what is in the box. Have them draw a picture of what they think the object looks like. This is their initial theory.

Next, tilt the box slowly side to side. Discuss the new facts that have been observed. Now the students draw a new picture of the object. Point out that this is an example of how scientists gain new knowledge as they have new techniques for learning.

Poke a small hole in the box and have a student use a pencil to poke at the object. Have the student share with the class the new facts that were gathered. Ask the students to change their drawings if the new facts suggest there should be a change.

Ask the students if they have any other ideas for ways to gather facts about the object without looking inside the box. Eventually you can let them look in the box. After you let them look inside the box, discuss that even if they did not figure out the exact object, as long as their theory fits the facts, they are on the right track.

This activity can be done as a class or have each student bring in their own mystery box to trade with a classmate.

Marble Boxes

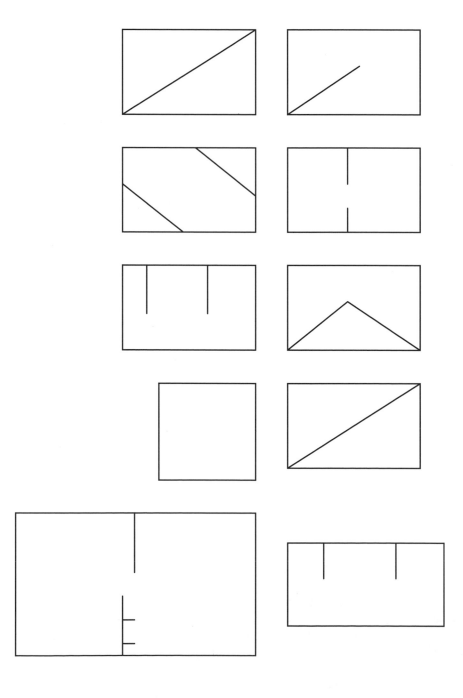

Materials: shoeboxes, marbles, tape, and cardboard

Inside each shoebox, use the tape and cardboard to create walls, for example. Then put a marble in the box and tape the top down. There should be one marble box for every two or three students.

Procedure:

Since scientists work together, students should work in groups as well. Tell your class there is a marble in the box and they should listen and feel as the marble rolls around to figure out how the cardboard walls in the box are arranged. The students can gently tilt the box back and forth to figure this out. Ask the students to first write down the facts they can observe about the arrangement of cardboard in the box. Based on these facts, they should draw a diagram of what they think it looks like in the box. After they open the box, discuss how well their facts fit their theories.

Puzzles

Jigsaw puzzles are another way to demonstrate the scientific process.

Materials: a puzzle

Procedure:

Hand out a few puzzle pieces to each child. The goal is to figure out what picture the puzzle makes when all the pieces are put together. Have the students write down the facts they observe that will help them figure out the picture. Even if the pieces do not fit together, what can be learned about the total puzzle? Pair the students up and ask them to write down what new facts they can gather now that there are more clues. Do they have any theories about what the puzzle creates? Now put the students into groups of four. Ask them to combine the pieces and gather more facts. Does this change or confirm their original theories? Repeat this step by putting the students into bigger groups to gather facts and discuss a theory. At this point, show them the picture of the completed puzzle. Discuss their theories. Even if they could not figure out just what the picture would look like, did their theory make sense? This is also another good opportunity to discuss the way scientists work together.

Now that the students have connected with the local environment and better understand how scientists learn, the next step is to understand the basic ecological principles needed to deal with environmental issues facing the world. This knowledge will give students what they need to understand about how the world works and how our actions can have a negative or positive effect.

Basic Ecological Concepts

Ecology is the study of the relationships and interactions living things have with each other and the non-living environment. The primary concept to get across to students is that everything is connected to something. Everything is dependent on something and nothing is completely independent. Everything affects something. Everything is affected by something. When we understand this, we realize that our actions matter. What we do has an impact; the choices we make can have positive or negative consequences. When we understand this basic concept of ecology, we can better understand how our world works and we can make better decisions by using this knowledge.

Here are the six principles of ecology adapted from the Center for Ecoliteracy. An understanding of these principles will be the groundwork for effective environmental action.

• Networks: Everything is interconnected in an intricate web of life where one thing affects another and nothing exists in isolation unaffected by anything else.

• Nested systems: In the natural world, many systems exist within another system, creating an interconnected, whole system.

• Cycles: The interrelationships of an ecosystem involve the cycles of the basic elements needed to sustain life. Thse cycles connect the land with the water and the atmosphere.

• Flows: All life is dependent on the flow of energy through the food cycle, starting with the sun.

• Development: Life changes at an individual, species, and ecosystem level.

• Dynamic balance: All interrelationships infuence each other in a dynamic balance that creates fluctuations.

Networks: What Am I Holding?

Materials: paper

Procedure:
Hold a sheet of paper in the air and ask "What am I holding?" Most students will simply say, "paper." Ask: "Is that all I am holding?" Prompt them a little more if they need it. Tell them that in fact you are holding water, soil, the wind that blew the tree seed, the trucks that brought the paper to the store, and more. Challenge them to come up with more of the interrelationships that helped to make the paper in your hands. As extra credit, they can do some reseach to find out more about how paper is made. Have them go home and ask family members the same question. The students can keep track of the responses and discuss what people thought.

Cycles

Food Cycle Game

Materials: outdoor space to run
Procedure:
This game is a fun way to learn the parts of a food cycle. Divide the children into two lines standing shoulder to shoulder facing each other about 15 feet apart. Mark home base lines about 20 yards behind each group. In the game, the students play the role of producers, consumers, or decomposers. Each part has a different symbol.

• Producers: The students reach for the sun and say "ahhhhhhh" because plants take sun, soil, air, and water, and produce food.

• Consumers: The students stretch their arms in front, opening and closing them like alligators, each time saying "chomp chomp." Animals can't make their own food; they need to eat other living things.

• Decomposers: The students wiggle their fingers and say "eeeeeeee." Decomposers live off dead plants and animals, thereby returning nutrients to the soil.

To play the game, each team huddles together and decides which role to play. The groups return to the starting line and face each other. On your signal, each group displays their symbols. Depending on the signal chosen, one group will chase the other. The activity is based on the game rock-paper-scissors. Producers chase decomposers (plants need good soil). Decomposers chase consumers (dead animals are decaycd into soil). Consumers chase producers (animals eat plants).

If both teams pick the same part, the teams return to the huddle and pick again. A student is caught if they are tagged before crossing the home base line. If caught, they join the other team, if not, they stay on the same side. Don't worry if it takes a few rounds for everyone to remember where to run.

Extensions:
After playing the game, search the schoolyard for signs of a food cycle in action.
Use dominoes to show how one one extinction can lead to another when animals are connected by a food chain. Label dominoes with the names of various local plants and animals. Have the students line the dominoes up in a creative pattern. By knocking down one of the dominoes, demonstrate how this sets off a chain reaction that affects many other parts of the ecosystem.
From: Kriesberg, Daniel A. *A Sense of Place: Teaching Children about the Environment with Picture Books.* Illustrated by Dorothy Frederick Englewood, CO: Teacher Ideas Press, 1999.

Carbon Cycle

The carbon cycle is just as important as the food cycle. All living organisms depend on carbon.

Materials: something to mark teams

Procedure:
Divide the class into three groups. One will be the producers, one the consumers, and one the decomposers. It is helpful to have have each group wear some sort of marker in order to tell them apart.

Carbon dioxide is one of the gases in our atmosphere. All living things need carbon. Plants can take carbon dioxide out of the air and use it to produce food for growth. Animals can't use the carbon dioxide directly so they eat plants or animals to get the carbon they need. When animals and plants die, the carbon is put back into the soil and air by decomposers. (Carbon is also returned to the atmosphere when animals breathe and when plant matter is burned, which is why burning fossil fuels contributes so much carbon dioxide, which is a greenhouse gas.)

In this game, leaves on the ground represent carbon. On your signal, producers run out and grab as many leaves as possible. As they run around picking up leaves, the consumers chase them. If a producer is tagged by a consumer, the producer gives all the leaves to the consumer and sits down for 15 seconds before reentering the game. Meanwhile, the decomposers are chasing either consumers or producers. If tagged by a decomposer, the leaves (carbon) are thrown back on the field and the student sits down for 15 seconds before reentering the game.

After the students are exhausted, ready to sit still and listen, you can review how carbon cycles through the environment. Hopefully, they have newfound respect for decomposers. Without the decomposers, carbon would be locked up in the dead producers and consumers and would be unavailable for new plants and animals. The amazing concept to understand is that it is the same carbon atoms that keep cycling through. The same carbon atoms that make up our bodies were in the bodies of living things millions of years ago. There is no waste, just the raw materials for the next step in the cycle.
From *Think Green, Take Action: Books and Activities for kids* by Daniel A. Kriesberg. Santa Barbara, CA: Libraries Unlimited. Copyright © 2010.

Nitrogen Cycle

The necessity of nitrogen for making protein makes this another key cycle for life to exist. The most common gas in our atmosphere is nitrogen. Seventy-eight percent of the air we breathe is nitrogen. All living things need nitrogen. The problem is that plants and animals can't use the nitrogen in the atmosphere unless it is changed into a different form. Fortunately, there is something that can do this: nitrogen-fixing bacteria, certain fungi, and blue-green algae. These organisms live in oceans, in the soil, and in the roots of legumes such as clover, peas, and beans. Once the nitrogen is converted by the bacteria, plants use it to grow, consumers get their nitrogen by eating plants, and the nitrogen is returned to the soil by decomposers when plants and animals die. In the soil, other bacteria change the nitrogen back into a form that is recycled into the air.

Materials: gram cubes or links

Procedure:
In this game, there will be five groups: nitrogen-fixing bacteria, producers, consumers, decomposers, and denitrifying bacteria. Spread out plastic links or gram cubes or anything else that can be connected together to represent nitrogen. The first group will be bacteria. They run out and connect as many markers as possible and put them back. The second group will be the producers. They run around looking for connected pieces of nitrogen. Consumers chase the producers and the decomposers chase the consumers or producers. Here the game is just like the the carbon cycle game except once the nitrogen is thrown back on the ground, there is another group of bacteria that breaks apart the connected pieces so the cycle can start again. After running around, they will be ready to discuss the implications of the nitrogen cycle.

From *Think Green, Take Action: Books and Activities for kids* by Daniel A. Kriesberg. Santa Barbara, CA: Libraries Unlimited. Copyright © 2010.

Water Cycle Juggling

Materials: index cards, ball

Procedure:
Another important cycle is the water cycle. Simply put, water is evaporated as a gas into the air by the sun. The water molecules move around the atmosphere and condense on particles of dust and fall to the earth as rain, snow, sleet, or other precipitation. The rain may fall either directly into a body of water and evaporate, or on the ground, where it can follow other paths through plants, soil, ice, and elsewhere. Eventually, the water ends up being evaporated again. The cycle has been going on since water was on Earth, with the same molecules circulating around and around.

To play, the children will represent the steps of a water cycle. The number of steps you use will depend on the number of students. The basic steps are sun, evaporation, clouds, ocean, river, and ground. If you have a group of 25 children, write each step six times on six different index cards. Pass all the cards out to the entire group. The children ask around and find everyone they need to create a complete set. If you have more students, make another set, or if you want larger groups, add more steps. For example, add a card for lakes, snow, ice, plants, humans, or wind.

Once the groups have been formed and the children are arranged in order and you have explained the basics of the water cycle, give each group a tennis ball to represent a water molecule. The goal is to pass the ball around the circle without dropping it. Since a water molecule can go from ocean to clouds or clouds to river or another combination, the children can throw the ball anywhere in the circle that follows the path of a water molecule. Since there is more than one path for a water molecule to take, anyone can throw the ball at evaporation. Clouds can throw to rivers, oceans, and ground. Ground can throw to ocean and river. While elements do move in a cycle, there are many pathways the elements may take in this journey. The students should call out the role they are playing and where they are throwing to further emphasize the steps of the water cycle. Add more tennis balls to each group to increase the challenge. It will be helpful to have vests or some other sign to mark who is who. Discuss the different paths the water molecules could take. Everyone will have to pay attention since the water molecules will not be following the same path twice. The lesson to learn from understanding all these cycles is the beauty of natural systems. There is no waste. What is used is reused. It is the same compounds now as then.

Flows: Energy in a Bucket

Materials: four buckets, six cups

Procedure:
Energy moves through the food chain beginning with the sun. Each living thing in the food chain takes in energy and gives out energy. Along the way, most of the original energy is lost. Most of it is used up at each level; in fact, only 10 percent is passed along to the next level.

You will need four buckets, two filled with water, and six cups. Poke one hole in the bottom of two cups and poke two holes in the bottom of two other cups and three holes in the last two cups. Divide the class into two relay teams. Put the buckets of water in front of each team. Put the empty bucket about 20 yards away. The water represents the energy from the sun. Plants are able to convert sunlight into usable energy for animals. Give the cup with one hole to the first person in each line. That cup represents plants. Give the second cup to another student. This cup represents a herbivore. This student stands in the middle between the two buckets. The third cup goes to a student who stands next to the empty bucket. This student represent a top-level carnivore. When you say "go," the plant scoops up some water, carries it to the herbivore, and pours it in the cup. Then the plant throws the cup back to the next student in line and waits in the herbivore's spot. Meanwhile, the herbivore carries the water to the carnivore and pours it into that cup and throws the empty cup back to the middle where the herbivore stands. Meanwhile, the carnivore then pours the remaining water into the empty bucket and throws the cup back to the herbivore spot and runs to the end of the line.

Continue the cycle until the plant energy bucket is empty. This game clearly shows how much energy is lost at each stage of the food chain. Gather the group together around the two buckets. Ask what happened to the energy. Most of the energy is not available for the animals to use. In a food chain, 90 percent of the energy is used up at each step. This fact has a significant effect on how many animals any particular habitat can support. This means a habitat has to have a large number of producers to have enough energy available for consumers. A top-level predator needs to have a lot of food resources in order to survive. One way to look at it in simplified terms is that it takes 1,000 plants to feed 100 mice, which feed 10 snakes, which feed one hawk, meaning the hawk needs 1,000 plants.

From *Think Green, Take Action: Books and Activities for kids* by Daniel A. Kriesberg. Santa Barbara, CA: Libraries Unlimited. Copyright © 2010.

Development

Tree Interview

Nature is in constant change—some changes we witness, some happen too fast or too slow to watch in time. It can be the slow change of geology or the rapid change of a hawk catching a mouse. When students look at a landscape, they are seeing only a snapshot in time. It has looked different and will look different. Ecological succession is the gradual change of one ecosystem into another. A field becomes a forest, or a pond becomes a wetland, or a stream becomes a pond. As the succession takes place, new plants and therefore new animals move in and others move out. An ecosystem that has habitats in various stages of succession has more diversity than one where there is only one stage.

Materials: access to a tree

Procedure:
To better understand these concepts, students can interview a tree. Find the biggest, oldest tree around. If possible, identify the species and estimate the age of the tree. Do a little research to find

out what the land was like around the tree 50 years ago, 100 years ago, and 150 years ago. Have the students present the information in the form of an interview with the tree, asking it what changes it has observed in the surrounding natural environment. If you only have a small tree available, it can relate the stories as if the parent tree told them.

What Would Happen If?

Materials: none

Procedure:
Ask the children to imagine what it would be like tomorrow if people left and there was no one to take care of the school. Have the students create a series of pictures of what the school would look like 50 years, 100 years, or 200 years in the future. How would the natural world develop and change? How would the school change?

Adaptations

Another important interrelationship to understand is between a living thing and its habitat. A habitat is the place where a living thing finds the food, water, and shelter it needs to survive. Every living thing also needs to protect itself from predators and from the elements in its habitat as well as reproduce. In order to do all these, living things are adapted to their habitats. An adaptation is what the living thing has or does that helps it to survive. The connection between adaptations and habitat is what allows the organism to survive; however, if the habitat is destroyed, the organism cannot simply change adaptations and survive in the new habitat. There is no longer a fit between the living organism and the habitat. Over time and generations, living organisms do change and develop as conditions change through the process of natural selection.

Materials: research resources

Procedure:
In order to learn some examples of adaptations, have the children pick an organism that is native to your area. Once they have selected their organism, they should try to answer the following questions:

• What is one adaptation your organism has to find food?

• What is one adaptation your organism has to protect itself from predators?

• What is one adaptation your organism has to protect itself from the local climate?

• What is one adaptation your organism has to help it reproduce?

• What is one other adaptation your organism has to survive?

Students can share the information by drawing a picture of their animal and labeling the adaptations.

Invent an Animal

This is a good project and a way to evaluate student understanding of the connection between habitat and place.

Materials: creative art supplies

Procedure:
Each child will invent and create a model of an animal or plant that is adapted to life in a child's bedroom. The first step is to study the habitat and observe the conditions. Before the students work on their own, lead them through a class example by inventing an animal that could survive in the bathtub.

Discuss the bathtub habitat. An animal or plant living in a bathtub would have to contend with a varying water supply that can leave the place dry for most of the day. The color of the habitat is white. Draining water has a great deal of suction. People come in on occasion. There very few other plants and animals. Ask the class to suggest ideas of adaptations that are needed to survive in a bathtub habitat. The animal will need adaptations to protect itself from weather conditions and local predators as well as for finding food, water, shelter, and for reproducing. Finally, the animal will need adaptations to reproduce. Some ideas may be suction cups to avoid being sucked down, white skin, and a piercing tongue to suck out toothpaste. After the students share their ideas, they need to invent an animal adapted to a child's bedroom. Discuss what would happen if their habitat was taken away.

If the habitat of an animal or plant is taken away, the animal or plant cannot simply move to a new place. If a forest becomes a field, a flying squirrel cannot just switch habitats. Only when a habitat changes very slowy over time can living organisms adapt by the process of natural selection.

From *Think Green, Take Action: Books and Activities for kids* by Daniel A. Kriesberg. Santa Barbara, CA: Libraries Unlimited. Copyright © 2010.

Nested Systems

Watershed Wonders

Watersheds are an example of a nested system; it is a system within a larger system. A watershed is the land surrounding a body of water that drains the water into that body of water. Watersheds connect to each other, and smaller watersheds are within bigger watersheds. Because watersheds connect land to water and water to land, it is important to look at the land through the eyes of the watershed instead of the separate parts. Because watersheds connect land and water over small and large distances, the cause of a problem can have its effect far downstream.

Tinfoil Mountains

Materials: tray, tinfoil, eyedropper, food coloring, and water

Procedure:
In the tray, students crumple up a sheet of tinfoil into the shape of a mountain range. Somewhere in their mountain range, they create a lake by cupping the foil into a bowl shape. Using the eyedropper, students drip water in different spots across the mountain range. They watch where the drops flow. Any part of the mountains that carries water into their lake is part of that lake's watershed. Drops that flow elsewhere are part of another watershed. As they drop more water on the mountains and the water flows into the tray, students can better understand how smaller watersheds are part of bigger watersheds.

What Is Your Watershed Address?
The students answer questions about their watershed address.

Materials: research resources

Procedure:
Assign two or three students to each question. Once they have found the answers, gather everyone together to share their knowledge.

• Where is the nearest body of water to the school?

• What is its name?

• What bigger watershed is your watershed part of?

• Are there any threats to your watershed?

• Where are some of the rivers or steams that flow through your watershed?

• Into what body of water does your watershed drain?

• How is your watershed connected to other watersheds?

• What political boundaries does your watershed cross?

Discuss: Why is it important to know your watershed?

For information on your watershed, you can go to the Environmental Protection Agency's "Surf Your Watershed" Web site, http://cfpub.epa.gov/surf/locate/index.cfm.

Dynamic Balance

Fox/Rabbit/Grass

This game shows the students an example of dynamic balance in nature.

Materials: open space

Procedure:
Set up the game in an open, grassy area. Have half of the students line up on one end as "grass" and the other half line up on the opposite end as "rabbits." In the middle, put two students to be "foxes." The roles change throughout the game so everyone will have a chance to play each role.

The game is played in a series of one-minute rounds. The rabbits will try to run across the field to grab a grass and run back to their shelter without being tagged by a fox. The grass and rabbits must hold hands as they run. If a fox tags a rabbit, the rabbit stands by you until the next round. The foxes continue to catch rabbits until the round ends. If a rabbit is tagged while holding a grass, the grass simply goes back to the line.

At the end of the round, any grass that made it back to the rabbit line is now a rabbit. Any rabbit that was tagged by a fox is now a fox. If a fox or rabbit did not tag a rabbit or get back with some grass, they did not get enough food to survive, so they become grass. Any rabbit that made it back is still a rabbit along with any grass that made it back with the rabbit.

Make sure each student is in the correct place at the end of each round. Note the population changes and dynamics as the game moves through several rounds. What happens if there are too many of any one population? How does each population affect the others? Discuss how the changes are going on. As an added feature, you can use Hula-hoops to make a safe zone to simulate hiding places for the rabbits.

With this understanding and connection to the natural world, students are equipped to understand and solve environmental problems.

Reference

Center for Ecoliteracy. "Principles of Ecology." http://www.ecoliteracy.org/education/principles_of_ecology.html.

CHAPTER 3

Endangered Species

Books

Baillie, Jonathon, and Marilyn Baillie. *Animals at the Edge.* Toronto: Maple Tree Press, 2008. 1897349335.

This book describes the work of the scientists in the Evolutionarily Distinct and Globally Endangered of Existence program that focuses on truly unique endangered species. The book highlights eight species and follows the scientists as they work to save these animals. The book is illustrated with photographs.

Base, Graeme. *Uno's Garden.* New York: Abrams Books for Young Readers, 2006. 1SBN 0:0-8109-5473-7.

This is a unique and stunning book with several different layers. The basic plot is the story of Uno and the beautiful forest he calls home. At first, there are a lot of creatures and few buildings, but as

time goes on, the number of buildings increases and the number of animals decreases. When all seems lost, there is hope, and a garden grows. It is also a counting book with patterns that record how the populations of animals and plants change with the advance of civilization. Students will enjoy searching the detailed illustrations for creatures hidden in the forest. Students can write their own counting books that show both how animals and plants can become endangered and how their populations can recover.

Batten, Mary. *Aliens from Earth*. Illustrated by Beverly J. Doyle. Atlanta, GA: Peachtree Publishers Ltd., 2008. 1561454508.

Non-native animals and plants are a major cause of extinction. The invasive species outcompete the native species for food, water, and shelter. Some invasive species prey on native animals as well. This book begins by explaining how the invasive species end up in the Untied States and why some places are more vulnerable than others. Some animals and plants came by accident while others were brought over on purpose. The illustrations will help readers identify invasive plants and animals in their own communities. The book ends with suggestions for preventing the spread of these invaders.

Cherry, Lynne. *The Dragon and the Unicorn*. New York: Gulliver Green Books, 1995. 0-15-224193-0.

This lavishly illustrated book is about a magical unicorn and the dragon it protects from danger. Their forest world is threatened when a king builds a fortress and sends his soldiers out to capture the unicorn in hopes of gaining its magic. The unicorn and dragon save themselves by showing the princess who then shows the king that the magic of the dragon is its wisdom of the forest. If the forest is destroyed, so is the wisdom.

Cole, Henry. *On Meadowview Street*. New York: Greenwillow Books, 2007. 0-06-056481-4.

Soon after Caroline has moved into her new home, her father starts mowing the lawn. She notices a flower growing right in the path of the mower. To save the flower, Caroline marks off the area with string. As more flowers, grow she continues to mark off more of the lawn. With each new protected area, more plants grow and more animals come. Eventually, her father sells the lawn mower, and their yard becomes a nature preserve. This book is a great way to start a habitat-rehabilitation project. Students will also enjoy finding the animals and plants hidden in the illustrations.

Collard, Sneed B. III. *Science Warriors: The Battle against Invasive Species.* Boston: Houghton Mifflin Company, 2008. 978-0-618-75636-0.

Invasive species destroy habitats and push native animals and plants toward extinction. In addition, they cause a large amount of economic damage to human interests. This book highlights the efforts of scientists as they try to figure out ways to prevent this from happening. The book is illustrated with photographs of invasive species and of scientists in action. The end of the book provides the readers with a number of ideas for helping to stop the spread of invasive species.

Cooper, Susan. *Green Boy.* New York: Simon and Schuster, 2002. 0-689-84751-3.

A combination of realistic and science fiction works to tell the story of Trey and his younger brother Lou. The setting is a small island in the Bahamas. The boys cross a barrier between the present and future into a land called Pangaea where they become involved in a fight to protect the land. Meanwhile, the small island they love to explore is being turned into a hotel resort. In both places, they become involved in the fight to preserve the land.

Cowcher, Helen. *Antarctica.* New York: Square Fish, 2009. 978-0312-589994.

This is the story of the emperor penguin and other animals that live in Antarctica. The book shows the natural challenges that make it hard to survive in such a harsh environment. The challenges only increase with the arrival of humans, who have come to build a base camp. Like the penguins and seals, the reader is left to wonder what will happen as more people come to Antarctica. The end of the book is a good prompt for a discussion about what will happen next in Antarctica and other remote places when humans arrive.

Cowley, Joy. *Video Shop Sparrow.* Illustrated by Gavin Bishop. Honesdale, PA: Boyd Mills Press, 1999. 1-56397-826-1.

It is New Year's Day, and Harry and George are returning a movie to the store. They see a sparrow trapped inside but the store is closed until January 13. There is no way to get in the store and save the bird. They go home but their parents are not much help and the police are not much help either. They even go to the mayor's house. The mayor is no help but they find someone who is.

DeFelice, Cynthia. *Lostman's River.* New York: Macmillan Publishing Company, 1994. 0-02726466.

This novel is set in the Everglades during the early 1900s where Tyler MacCauley lives with his family. He meets a man named Mr. Strawbridge who wants to hire Tyler to guide him through the Everglades searching for wildlife to observe and study. Instead, deep in the swamp at the heron rookeries, Mr. Strawbridge shoots some herons and egrets. More problems develop when other men arrive to hunt the birds for their feathers. They kill Mr. Strawbridge, find the rookeries, and shoot all the birds. Tyler escapes but knows that he will someday return to save the rest of the birds.

Fern, Tracey E. *Buffalo Music.* Illustrated by Lauren Castillo. New York: Clarion Books, 2008. 978-0-618-72341-6.

Once the buffalo hunts began it did not take long for the enormous herds to become just a few scattered individuals. The book was inspired by the true story of Mary Ann Goodnight, who along with her husband was among the first people to recognize that buffalo were endangered. They raised a captive herd of buffalo that later became the foundation for the reestablishment of buffalo in Yellowstone National Park and other places. Thankfully, there were people like Molly who loved to listen to the music of the buffalo.

George, Jean Craighead. *Everglades*. Illustrated by Wendell Minor. New York: HarperCollins, 1995. 0-06-021228-4.

A storyteller takes five children out into the Everglades and tells them about this truly unique and beautiful place. He takes them into the past to show how the Everglades came to be and all the wildlife that lived there. The children also learn what happened as more people came to the Everglades. The children are saddened by the story, so the storyteller tells them a new one. This is about the five children who grew up and "ran the world" and brought the Everglades back to life. Wendell Minor's illustrations are stunning.

Graham, Bob. *How to Heal a Broken Wing*. Cambridge, MA: Candlewick Press, 2008. 978-0-7636-3903-7.

In a big city where no one is paying attention, a bird breaks a wing and falls to the sidewalk. A young boy named Will is the only one to see it. Along with his understanding parents, they take they bird home and help it to heal. Although the pigeon they rescue is not an endangered species, the book still is a wonderful way to teach about wildlife rehabilitation. It is a story powerfully told with few words and wonderful illustrations.

Hiaasen, Carl. *Hoot*. New York: Alfred A. Knopf, 2002. 0-375-82181-3.

This great novel combines ecological adventure with the perils of middle school. Roy has just moved to Florida from Montana and is having trouble fitting in. He befriends a mysterious boy who along with his stepsister is trying to stop a restaurant chain from building a new pancake house where burrowing owls are nesting. Roy and his friends are able to stop the restaurant from being built with the creative use of protest and the media. The book has a lot of potential for discussing topics such as endangered species, nonviolent protest, bullies, and life in middle school.

Hobbs, Will. *Jackie's Wild Seattle*. New York: Harper Collins, 2003. 0-688-17474-4.

This novel about 14-year-old Shannon and her younger brother Cody begins as they are spending the summer in Seattle with their uncle who works at an animal-rehabilitation center. They become involved in lots of adventures as they rescue raccoons, eagles, seals, and more. Shannon also learns that relationships with family and friends are more complicated than they seem.

Jackson, Donna. M. *The Wildlife Detectives: How Forensic Scientists Fight Crimes against Nature*. Photographs by Wendy Shattil and Bob Rozinski. Boston: Houghton Mifflin, 2000. 0-395-86976-5.

When an elk is illegally shot in Yellowstone National Park, a team of detectives from the Fish and Wildlife Service arrive on the scene to figure out who committed the crime. The book tells the story step-by-step as the scientists solve the mystery and find the man who shot the elk. Sidebars provide information on poaching and other animal crimes. Even the glossary at the end is a way to grab the reader's interest.

Jenkins, Steve. *Almost Gone: The World's Rarest Animals*. New York: HarperCollins, 2006. 0-06-053600-4.

Wonderfully illustrated by the author, this book features the most endangered animals of the world. For each animal, there are illustrations, the remaining population, and information on the animal's habits and the reasons it is on the brink of extinction. For some animals, there is a tiny bit of hope, but for others, it may be too late.

Johnson, Sylvia, *A Raptor Rescue! An Eagle Flies Free*. Photographs by Ron Winch. New York: Dutton Children's Books, 1995. 0-525-45301-6.

This nonfiction book tells the story of the patients at the Gabbert Raptor Center, where as many as 600 raptors are treated for injuries. The focus of the book is on one injured bald eagle that was given surgery and eventually reintroduced into the wild. This book can also be used to feature one of the many jobs in the environmental field. It is thrilling to see how an eagle goes from injury to regaining the freedom of flight.

Jordan, Rosa. *The Last Wild Place*. Atlanta, GA: Peachtree Publishing, 2008. 978-1-56145-458-7.

Chip and Luther are best friends and like all friends have their ups and downs, especially when so many changes are happening in their families. As an escape, Chip goes to the woods behind his farm and finds a family of panthers. When developers threaten to destroy the forest, Chip and Luther stand up for the panthers and stop the development. An interesting sidelight is Chip's science teacher and the way he uses journals to teach in the outdoors.

Kleven, Elisa. *The Dancing Deer and the Foolish Hunter*. New York: Dutton Juvenile, 2002. 0525468323.

This is a beautifully illustrated book that shows animals need their own habitat. A hunter captures a deer that can dance and decides to sell him to the circus. The hunter learns the deer cannot dance without being in the forest. Even when the hunter tries to re-create the forest in his house by bringing parts of it home, the deer will not dance. Finally, the hunter realizes the deer needs all parts of the forest as much as he does. There are also many small details to the illustrations that subtly point out the problems of overconsumption.

Markle, Sandra, and William Markle. *Gone Forever! An Alphabet of Extinct Animals*. Illustrated by Felipe Davalos. New York: Simon and Schuster, 1998. 1416061380.

This alphabet book is illustrated with bold, realistic paintings of a variety of extinct animals. Along with each illustration is text that explains some of the interesting habits of each animal and how humans caused their extinction. After reading this book, ask students how they would classify all the various causes of extinction. The back of book has a message about how to help endangered species. This book works for all ages to introduce them to the wide variety of animals that have become extinct.

McLimans, David. *Gone Wild: An Endangered Animal Alphabet*. New York: Walker and Company, 2006.

This Caldecott Honor book is a great introduction to the diversity of endangered species. The black-and-white illustrations boldly combine each letter with a graphic design of the animal. Each illustration is accompanied by information on the animal's habitat, range, threats, and status. The back of the book includes more interesting information on each of the animals.

Mendoza, George. *Were You a Wild Duck, Where Would You Go?* Illustrated by Jan Osborn-Smith. New York: Workman Publishing, 1990. 1-55670-136-5.

Absolutely beautiful watercolor illustrations grace this book that tells the story of a mallard duck. The poetic language describes its search from place to place as it is witness to the loss of habitat along the way. The book ends with hope that the land will be saved. The mallard asks, "Who will sing my song with me?" He is answered by children, who say, "We are the children who can soar above the greed of our day."

Nirgiotis, Nicholas, and Theodore Nirgiotis. *No More Dodos: How Zoos Help Endangered Species*. Minneapolis, MN: Lerner Publications Company, 1996. 0-8225-2856-8.

This is an in-depth resource that explains how zoos are working to save endangered species. The book opens with the successful captive breeding program that helped save the black-footed ferret from extinction. The book also explains how zoos have become more aware of animals' natural habitats so they can create enclosures that will lead to successful breeding. There is also information on some of the challenging issues faced by people saving these animals. There is the important message that no matter how successful zoos are, if the environment is damaged, then animals can't be saved.

Pratt-Serafini, Kristin Joy. *The Forever Forest: Kids Save a Tropical Treasure*. Illustrated by Kristin Joy Pratt-Serafini. Nevada City, CA: Dawn Publications, 2008. 978-1-58469-101-3.

In 1987, first- and second-grade students from a school in Sweden began raising money to purchase rain forest land in Costa Rica. Their goal was to save 25 acres. The word spread, more people became involved, more money was raised, and more land was protected. In fact, 54,000 acres have been protected in what is now called the Children's Eternal Rainforest. This book tells the story of Peter's visit to the Costa Rican forest with his mother. Besides seeing and learning about the amazing wildlife, he finds out his mother was one of the children who helped save the rain forest. Sidebars have information about amazing rain forest plants and animals and how the work of seven- and eight-year-olds continues to spread all over the world.

Priebe, Mac. *The Peregrine Falcon—Endangered No More*. Illustrations by Jennifer Priebe. Norwalk, CT: Mindfull Publishing, 2000. 0-9669551-9-6.

The recovery of the peregrine falcon from near extinction is truly an environmental success story. By banning DDT and beginning a captive breeding program, the peregrine falcon population has recovered. This book, part of the Wildlife Winners series, explains how the recovery program worked. Falcon facts on each page add interesting information. The photographs capture the power of this stunning bird.

Smith, Marie, and Toland, Smith. *Z is for Zookeeper*. Illustrated by Henry Cole. Chelsea, MI: Sleeping Bear Press, 2005. 1-58536-158-5.

This is an alphabet book that shows the varied aspects of being a zookeeper by explaining the different jobs a zookeeper must do. For example, in "R is for records," zookeepers must keep records on everything the animals do throughout the week. On one side of each page is more detailed information on record-keeping. This pattern is followed for each letter along with bright illustrations.

Swinburne, Stephen. *Once a Wolf: How Wildlife Biologists Fought to Bring Back the Gray Wolf*. Photographs by Jim Brandenburg. Boston: Houghton Mifflin, 1999. 0-395-89827-7.

The story of the reintroduction of the wolves into Yellowstone National Park is a demonstration of how saving one species benefits an entire ecosystem. Wolves were hunted close to extinction in the lower 48 states. With the passage of the Endangered Species Act, efforts slowly began to reintroduce wolves to Yellowstone. The author details how biologists proceeded and the challenges they faced from people who opposed the wolf reintroduction. The program has continued to be successful, and the Yellowstone ecosystem is now back in balance.

Toft, Kim Michelle, and Allan Sheather. *One Less Fish*. Illustrated by Kim Michelle Toft. Watertown, MA: Charlesbridge Publishing, 1998. 10987654321.

Set in a coral reef, this counting book goes from 12 down to zero as one fish is taken away at a time because of the many problems facing the coral reefs. For example, "nine tiny triggerfish wonderfully ornate. One found a plastic bag and now there are eight." After each rhyme there is background information that explains the problem in more detail. The brightly colored illustrations capture the amazing beauty of the coral reef as well as any photograph can. While the book counts down to zero, the last pages describe the ways people are working to protect the coral reef.

Ward, Helen. *The Tin Forest*. Illustrated by Wayne Anderson. New York: Dutton Children Books, 2001. 0-525-4687-4.

This is an interesting take on what can happen with a dream and a breadcrumb. An old man who lives next to a garbage dump dreams of living in a forest filled with animals. He builds a forest out of the garbage, complete with animals made from metal and other materials. One day he drops a crumb from his sandwich and a real bird flies in and takes it. He makes a wish, and the bird returns and drops seeds on the ground. Real plants grow, and more animals come. The old man's wish has come true.

Activities

Introduction

Extinction is a natural process, and throughout time, living organisms have become extinct. It is a part of the ongoing evolution through natural selection in which some species become extinct and others survive due to a changing world. Now, however, extinction rates have increased dramatically because of human activity. In North America alone biologists believe that since 1625, more then 500 species of plants and animals have become extinct. Around the world, the number is much higher. Habitat destruction, overconsumption for commercial benefit, pollution, and invasive species are all factors that have caused the extinction of thousands of plants and animals and have pushed many others to the brink. We have identified only a small percentage of the living organisms on Earth. There are still thousands of unidentified species. At current rates of extinction, the Earth is losing these animals and plants before we even know they exist. Fortunately, more and more people recognize the problem of extinction and endangered species and are taking steps to prevent this loss from continuing.

There are many reasons why we should make the effort and spend the time and money to save endangered species.

Biodiversity: All living things are connected in a network of interrelationships that create a complex web of interdependence. The extinction of one living organism will affect other species. Since many living organisms are in symbiotic relationships, the extinction of one can cause the extinction of another. The web of life is supported by diverse forms of life; each extinction weakens the web.

Medicine: All forms of life are storehouses of genetic material. This genetic material has provided us with many of the medicines we use today. For example, a fungus gave us penicillin. More than a quarter of all prescriptions written each year in the United States contain chemicals discovered in plants and animals. Only a small fraction of the living things on Earth have been studied for their medicinal values. Once an organism becomes extinct, the genetic materials are gone forever. If we lose the animal or plant, we may also be losing a valuable drug.

Agriculture: Many of our crops are dependant on insects and other living things to help with pollination, seed dispersal, soil fertility, and to combat pests. The extinction of one of these beneficial organisms may affect our food supply. In addition, there may be an undiscovered plant that could be a new source of food.

Environmental monitors: Certain species are very sensitive to changes in the environment. These species act as a warning to us that something could eventually negatively affect our lives as well. The rapid decline in the population of freshwater mussels was an early indicator that the river waters in the eastern United States were becoming polluted.

Ecosystem services: The world's ecosystems supply the Earth with water and air. They decompose waste and cycle key compounds such as carbon and nitrogen. Human beings and all life depend on these services. We don't pay for them, but we rely on them. If we allow animals and plants to become extinct, we may lose the species that help these ecosystems services work.

Economic values and recreation: People like to watch wildlife; they go on vacations to see wild-life, and they buy camera equipment, binoculars, and hire guides to take tours. Wildlife watching in the United States generated $85 billion in economic benefits in 2001. This spending helps support a great many businesses.

The inherent value of life: Perhaps the most important reason we should work to stop the extinction of living things is that they have an inherent right to life, and who are we to end it?

The first step in saving endangered species is for scientists to recognize if a species is in decline by tracking its population. Scientists have to be able to identify the plant, animal, or other forms of life in order to estimate their populations. In addition, scientists have to study the living organism in order to understand how it lives and its interconnections with the rest of the world. With this knowledge, scientists can find out how best to help endangered species recover and survive.

Recognizing Endangered Species

Identifying Plants and Animals

The first step to protecting endangered species is to recognize them and be aware of the animal or plant's population. In order to count who and what lives in a given area, scientists need to learn the names of the organisms. Here are two activities to help students meet their animal and plant neighbors. By being able to identify plants and animals, students will develop more awareness and be more observant of changes in their populations. It is the same as when we know the names of other people, we pay closer attention to them and we want get to know them better and take care of them.

Tree Key

Materials: copy of tree key for each student

Procedure:
Make copies of the tree key below and take the students outside to identify the evergreen trees in your schoolyard. Identification keys work as a series of questions leading to the answer. For example, students observe an evergreen tree and first ask: "Are the leaves needle-like or scale-like?" Depending on the answer, they go to step 2 or step 10. Continue to ask these questions to figure out which step to go to next. Now the students can identify the trees in the schoolyard and around the neighborhood. Discuss which trees are common, rare, threatened, and endangered in the community. If you cannot take students outdoors, you can bring some branches and give them a chance to practice keying out the species.

Key to Common Evergreens

1. leaves needle-like	go to step 2
1. leaves scale-like	go to step 10
2. needles in bundles on the stem	go to step 3
2. needles single on the stem	go to step 7
3. needles in bundles of twos	go to step 4
3. needles in bundles of threes or fives	go to step 6
4. needles $1/4$ inch to $2^1/2$ inches, long and twisted	Scotch Pine
4. needles $2^1/2$ to 6 inches long, not twisted	go to step 5
5. needles slender, snap when bent double	Red Pine
5. needles stout, do not snap when bent double	Austrian Pine
6. needles in threes	Pitch Pine
6. needles in fives	White Pine
7. needles angular, stiff, easily rolled between thumb and finger	Spruce
7. needles flat, not stiff, not easily rolled between thumb and finger	go to step 8
8. needles with sharply pointed tip, all green underneath	Yew
8. needles with blunt tip, often with white lines underneath	go to step 9
9. needles $1/2$ inch to $1/4$ inch, cones $1/4$ inch	Hemlock
9. needles more than $1/4$ inches long, cones more than $1^1/2$ inches long	Fir
10. flattened branchlets, fan-like, needles scale like	Arborvitae (eastern white cedar)
10. branchlets cord-like, needles sharply pointed	Juniper or Red Cedar

Indoor/Outdoor Bird Watching

Knowing our neighbors is not limited to plants; it is good to know some of the animals that live in our community. Birds are a great subject to study since there are many species that live in urban and suburban areas. They are mainly diurnal, which means they are active in the daylight hours just as we are.

Materials: pictures of birds, field guides

Procedure: Make a list of 10 common bird species living in your community. You can consult the local Audubon Society for assistance as to which birds live in your area. Find a picture of each bird in a magazine, on a Web site, or via another resource. All About Birds, a Web site from the Cornell Lab of Ornithology has great information on birds, at http://www.allaboutbirds.org/NetCommunity/Page.aspx?pid=1189.

Enature.com is another Web site that has online field guides for birds and many other groups of animals at http://www.enature.com/home/.

Before showing the pictures, ask the students what characteristics of birds will help to identify them besides color. Body shape, posture, size, shape of bill, feet, wing shapes, songs, flight patterns, and habitat preferences all help to identify birds.

Spread the photos out on a table. Have the students number a sheet of paper 1–10. Hand out bird identification books and let the children try to identify the birds using the field guides. Petersen First Guides and Audubon Society First Field Guides are perfect for students. Remind them not to depend solely on the pictures in the book; they also need to read the text to make sure the information makes sense for the bird they are trying to identify. Give the students time to identify as many birds as possible.

Next, hold up each picture and ask the class if anyone can identify the bird. As you go through the birds, point out some of the identifying characteristics of each and some of their interesting habits. Later, you can test the students by holding up the picture and having the students call out or write down their answers. I like to move the pictures around as if the bird is flying to make it more of a realistic challenge.

As the children spend time outdoors, they should keep track of which birds they see on campus and in their neighborhoods. Tally up all the sightings of each bird and discuss the population status. While these birds are not endangered, it is a good way of starting the discussion about why populations vary.

Animal Signs

Scientists cannot always see the animals they are looking for. They often have to find signs left behind to know that the animal is living in the area. This is a good activity to do at home.

Materials: scavenger-hunt sheets

Procedure:

To find animal signs, students will have to be very observant and look and listen all around. If this activity is done on a regular basis year after year, the information can be graphed and used to look for patterns in animal populations. Take the students for a walk outdoors and see how many of the signs they can find on the following list:

An animal track _____

A feather _____

A bird nest _____

A leaf eaten by an insect _____

Droppings _____

An insect nest _____

A dead animal _____

A piece of fur _____

An actual animal _____

Tunnels _____

Animal sounds _____

Holes in a tree _____

Holes in the ground _____

How Many Are There?

To protect endangered species we need to know what living organisms are endangered. To do this, scientists need to know the population of an organism. Population is defined as the number of individuals of a species in a given area. By knowing the populations scientists have the baseline data they need to make comparisons year to year on the growth, decline, or stability of the population.

Counting Plants

Materials: metersticks, craft sticks, or something else that can be used to mark out a square

Procedure:
Take the students to a lawn and mark off an area about 15 meters by 5 meters. Ask them how they could estimate the number of clovers (or select a different plant besides grass) that is growing on the lawn. Discuss their ideas to estimate the population of the plants.

One simple and effective method is to count the number of clovers in one square meter and multiply that by the total area of the lawn. Give each group of 2-4 students a meterstick and four craft sticks. Each group will mark out a square that is one meter by one meter and count how many clovers are in the square. They should pick their squares at random to avoid any bias. Once all the groups are done counting, find the average number of clover per square meter for all the squares the students counted. To get an estimate of the entire population, the students simply multiply the average number of clovers per square meter with the area of the lawn. Discuss what they could do to make a more accurate estimate. Discuss how scientists can use this information to ensure a healthy population of the plant.

Animal Populations

Plants do not move, which makes it easier to estimate their populations than animals. Most animals move, but scientists can still estimate their populations without counting the same animal twice by using the catch-and-release method. Animals are captured and marked in a manner that does not hurt them and then released. Animals continue to to be captured and counted. When an unmarked animal is captured, the scientist marks the animal. When a previoulsy marked animal is caught, the scientists simply record the recapture. Since capturing and releasing wild animals is not possible for most classes, your students can participate in the following simulation.

Materials: toothpicks, paper bags

Procedure:
Empty a box of toothpicks into a paper bag to represent animals in their habitat. To capture animals, the students reach in the bag and pull out a small handful of toothpicks. They mark the toothpicks with a pen and count the number of toothpicks, then they release them back into the bag. The students shake the bag and then pull out another small handful of toothpicks. The formula for estimating animal populations by marking the captured animals is easy to use. Population estimate over capture one total equals capture two total over recaptures.

Estimated population is X:

$$\frac{X}{\text{capture one}} = \frac{\text{capture two}}{\text{recaptures}}$$

For example:

$$\frac{X\ (110)}{\text{captures }(31)} = \frac{\text{capture two }(25)}{\text{recaptures }(7)}$$

Biodiversity

Another measure used by scientists to determine the status of living organisms is biodiversity. Biodiversity is all the number of different species of living organisms in a given area. In most cases, the greater the biodiversity, the more stable and healthier the ecosystem.

Materials: metersticks

Procedure:
On the school grounds, students measure and mark a one meter by one meter square. Within the square, the students count how many different species of plants and animals they find. They do not need to know the name of the plant or animal; it is okay to make up a descriptive name to identify and remember the plant or animal. They also need to count or estimate the population of each living organism they find.

Diversity equals the total number of species divided by total number of individuals. Take the students to other places on campus and have them repeat the procedure. Pick places that are less impacted by human activities and compare them to places where there is more human activity. Find the biodiversity for plants and the biodiversity for animals separately. Is there a pattern in which the higher the diversity of plants leads to a higher diversity of animals? If so, what does that teach us about helping to protect wildlife?

Students can try this at home as well.

Big Map of Where

Materials: blank map of the world or the United States

Procedure:
On a large wall map, mark the places where endangered species live. This can be part of the research students are doing or an activity itself. As different endangered species are added to the map, discuss the following questions:

Which places are home to most endangered species?

What patterns do you observe?

Then and Now

Materials: research resources, blank maps

Procedure:
Ask the students to select an endangered plant or animal and research its former range. On a blank map, color the former range green. Now color the current range red. How much has it changed? The class can focus on one continent or the entire world. Go to Worldatlas.com for blank maps at http://www.worldatlas.com/webimage/testmaps/maps.htm.

Causes

There are four major reasons why animals, plants, and other living organisms become extinct or endangered. The number one cause of extinction and endangered species is habitat destruction. Other causes include pollution, invasive species, and overconsumption for economic reasons. A species can also become extinct or endangered because of a combination of these factors. One factor may push the organism to the edge and another pushes it over. Animals and plants that are most at risk have some of the following characteristics:

Competition with humans: Some animals and plants require the same habitat that is desired by humans and they lose out.

Size: Animals that are large need large habitats which can put them in conflict with humans.

Migration patterns: Animals that migrate over long distances are vulnerable because they need to be able to find food, water, and shelter over a very wide area.

Naturally low populations: Some animals and plants have a low population for reasons outside of human control. Even a slight decrease in population from human causes can lead to extinction.

Environmental sensitivity: Some animals and plants are very sensitive to small changes in their habitat. If human actions cause even a slight difference in the health of the habitat, the animal or plant may become endangered.

Breeding habits: Animal and plants that reproduce slowly have a difficult time regaining their populations if human activity has caused too many of them to die off.

Food and nesting habits: If the animals can live only on certain foods or have other specific dietary needs, they are more likely to become endangered since they cannot easily adapt to changing conditions.

Desirable: The plant or animal has something people want, such as fur, flowers, food, or medicinal value.

Invasive Species

Plant and Animal Invaders

Animals, plants, and other living things that have spread beyond the places where they are native are called non-native species or invasive species. Due to human activities, there are many animals and plants that live in new places. Invasive plants crowd out native species by outcompeting them for soil, sun, and water. This can set off a chain reaction if the native plant that is crowded out is the food source of a certain insect. That insect is now threatened, and the animal that ate the insect is also now in trouble. Invasive animals can inflict a high degree of predation on native animals that are not adapted to protect themselves from the invasive animal. Invasive species come to these new places accidentally; for example, seeds of some plant species get mixed up in soil being transported overseas, or an insect may have laid its eggs in lumber that is being sold in another country. There are also invasive species that people introduced with the idea that their presence would be beneficial, only to find out that these species reproduced rapidly and caused a great deal of environmental harm.

Wanted Posters

Materials: paper and art supplies

Procedure:
Students make wanted posters of invasive species in their community so that others can identify the plant or animal and help slow their spread. The posters should include the name of the invasive species, a drawing of the invasive species, and a photograph of it. Briefly explain the problems that the invasive species causes. Explain how people can help to solve the problem.

This Web site from the United States Department of Agriculture's National Invasive Species Center has a lot of helpful information about a variety of invasive species: http://www.invasive speciesinfo.gov/unitedstates/state.shtml.

Pollution

Pollution causes problems for living organisms is many ways. Toxic wastes and pesticides can kill them directly or cause reproductive problems. Other types of pollution, such as acid precipitation and nitrogen-loading, change the chemistry of the water, air, or land, making it difficult for life to continue.

Bioaccumulation Game

Bioaccumulation is the way small amounts of pollution can become concentrated in the bodies of animals, causing them harm.

Materials: about 50 craft sticks

Procedure:
To prepare the game, mark half the craft sticks with a black line, which represents toxic chemicals in the food chain. However, do not tell the students why some of the sticks have black marks. Set clear boundaries for this version of tag. The craft sticks represent food. Divide your class into the three groups. Depending on the size of your class, put about twelve students in one group that will be small fish, another group of about seven will be big fish, and make the third group osprey with about three students. Throw the food sticks out over the grass. The small fish run out first and gather up as many food sticks as they can. Count to ten and send the big fish out to catch little fish. If a big fish tags a small fish, the food sticks are passed along to the big fish and the little fish is out of the game. After all the little fish are eaten, send out the osprey. They chase the big fish. When a big fish is tagged, the food sticks are passed to the osprey.

Once all the fish are caught, gather the students around. Ask the osprey how many sticks they have with a black mark. If they have three or more, that means that the osprey has accumulated enough DDT to cause the females to lay eggs with shells so thin that they crack when the ospreys sit on them. This is what happened to osprey between the 1950s and 1970s.

You can repeat the game by changing the groups to little fish, tuna fish, and humans to show how we are part of the food chain and can be affected by pollutants in the environment.

An indoor version of this game can be played by first putting the craft sticks around the classroom. The little fish search the room, collecting fish. The bigger fish go up to the little fish and instead of chasing them and tagging them, they play rock-paper-scissors. If the big fish wins, the little fish gives the food stick to the big fish. If the big fish loses, it has to find another little fish. Eventually, when all or almost all of the little fish have been eaten, send in the osprey. They also play rock-paper-scissors to catch a big fish.

Overconsumption

Overconsumption for economic reasons has caused the extinction of many animals. People hunt animals for food, folk medicines, pets, furs, and trophies. Some wild plants are overharvested for their flowers, medicinal value, and for food. Even when these plants and animals are protected by law, they suffer from poaching by people who hunt and gather them illegally.

How Much Can We Take?

Materials: plastic cubes

Procedure:
This activity demonstrates what happens when people take too much. The cubes will represent fish that people are catching to sell. The goal of the game is to grab 10 cubes (fish) to earn money. To make the game a bit more realistic and to add motivation, you can have students trade in their 10 cubes for a prize, for example, some candy or a coupon for a night free of homework.

To play the game, divide the students into groups of 10 or so. Place 20 cubes (fish) on the floor and have the first group make a circle around the cubes. The students from the other group simply observe how the first group handles the task and then they will have a turn.

Rules:

1. Students need 10 cubes (fish).
2. Each round lasts 15 seconds.
3. If there are any cubes left over at the end of the round, one cube will be added for each cube that remains.
4. When all the cubes are gone, the game is over.

On "go," the students try to get 10 cubes. Usually they will just grab and there will be nothing left. If any cubes are left in the circle after a round is over, add one cube for each one that is still left. (The fish were able to reproduce.) If there are no cubes left, then the game is over since there were no more fish left to reproduce.

Most likely after the first try there will be one person with 10 cubes and all the others will be gone but no one will have enough fish to earn money. The game is over. Now give the next group a chance. Most likely the same thing will happen. The students will grab the cubes as quickly as they can, leaving none behind, and the game will be over.

Ask students if they want one more chance. At this point, some of them may begin to realize that if they take a few cubes at a time and leave some of the cubes behind, more cubes will be added. If they continue this process, everyone can have enough cubes for a prize, and there will even be cubes left over for future generations and the fish will not become extinct.

Discuss:

How did it feel when only a couple of people had enough cubes to get a prize?

Why did it take more than one round to figure out the best way to do this?

How come sometimes even when we know what we should do, we still do not do it?

How does this apply to the real world?

What are some examples of this happening in the world today? In the past?

How can we prevent overconsumption?

Habitat Destruction

Understanding habitat destruction is simple: every living thing needs a place to live. If that place is destroyed, the living thing will die. Each organism has special adaptations that allow it to survive in a particular habitat. Organisms cannot just switch to a new habitat if the old one is destroyed.

Green Space Survey

Materials: maps of your community

Procedure:
Either draw or find a map of your community. Color in all the open space green. Using old maps, local historical society and government records, and interviews with older members of the community, the students find out the history of land development in the community. They can then draw a series of maps that show the changes in open space as time has passed.

The students can discuss what has changed in their own neighborhoods in their lifetimes. The main causes of habitat destruction are construction, development, agriculture, forestry, mining, and pollution. What examples of each of these can students find in their community?

Habitat-Loss Game

Materials: paper plates, dice

Procedure:
The plates represent the habitat the endangered species needs to survive. Spread the plates on the floor in the classroom or on the ground outside. To begin, each student stands on one of the paper plates. Since the game represents habitat destruction, the teacher will be rolling dice to decide what event will cause the loss of the animals' habitat. While this explanation of the game works for a typical endangered species, the game has more of an impact if you can use the specific issues facing an endangered species that lives in the same area of the country as the students.

The game begins with each student standing on a plate and a few extra plates scattered around. Roll the dice. The number rolled determines how many plates are taken away and the cause of habitat destruction. For example, if a four is rolled, four plates will be taken away because of poor farming practices. After each roll, the students bring all the plates to you; take out four plates explaining that in this case, poor farming practices are causing erosion. The students then close their eyes while you put the remaining plates out. On "go," they run out and try to find a plate. Anyone who does not find a plate "dies" and is out of the game. Repeat this until there are only one or two students left. As the population dwindles, discuss the following vocabulary words:

Vanishing: A species that is decreasing in population

Extinct: A species that has no surviving members, there are no more alive anywhere

Extirpated: A species that is absent in one area but may exist in another

Endangered: A species that is in danger of becoming extinct

Here are some general suggestions of events that can happen to the animal you can use for playing the game:

Roll a 1: A new housing development is built; take away one habitat plate.

Roll a 2: Invasive species push out food resources; take away two habitat plates.

Roll a 3: Trees are cut down to produce paper products; take away three habitat plates.

Roll a 4: Poor farming practices have caused erosion to wash away topsoil; take away four plates.

Roll a 5: A stream is diverted to use the water for industry; take away five habitat plates.

Roll a 6: A new highway is built; take away six habitat plates.

Keep playing until there are no more habitat plates and the last animal is gone. However, another way to play is to stop the habitat destruction before all the animals are gone. When two or three students are remaining, change the game so that depending on the number rolled, the habitat is restored.

Here are some general events that can be used for adding plates through habitat restoration:

Roll a 1: The animal is placed on the endangered species list for added protection.

Roll a 2: An educational campaign is begun to teach people how to improve their backyard habitat.

Roll a 3: Breeding grounds are preserved as a national wildlife refuge.

Roll a 4: There will be a road project with safe animal crossing areas.

Roll a 5: Invasive plants are removed to restore the habitat.

Roll a 6: Development is halted in the animal's habitat.

The game is more meaningful if you use an endangered species from where the children live. Check the environmental conservation offices for your state about endangered species in your area. Find out what threats are causing the animal to become endangered and what is being done to help it. Use this to make the game fit the animal or plant. Here is an example using the piping plover.

Piping Plover:

Threats:
Roll a 1: Development on beaches and shorelines takes away nesting habitats.
Roll a 2: Cats and dogs harass birds on nests and eat eggs and chicks.
Roll a 3: Vehicle driving on beaches destroys nests.
Roll a 4: New housing developments attract raccoons and other suburban predators that eat eggs and chicks.
Roll a 5: Increases in the number of beachgoers harasses the birds.
Roll a 6: Erosion of beaches takes away the nesting habitat.

There are ways that people are helping the population to recover.
Roll a 1: Fencing around nesting areas keeps people from disturbing the nests.
Roll a 2: Signs and other forms of education help people understand why it is important to leave the birds alone.
Roll a 3: An education program explains to people that keeping their cats indoors protects the birds.
Roll a 4: Institute and enforce leash laws in order to keep dogs from running loose and scaring birds.
Roll a 5: Institute and enforce a ban on cars, ATVs, and other vehicles from driving on the beach.
Roll a 6: Research piping plovers to learn more about their lifestyle.

Population Growth of Humans

With more and more people, there is less and less room for many animals and plants. The dramatic increase in the human population has a direct impact on other forms of life on Earth.

Materials: chart

Procedure:
Use the chart to make a graph visually depicting the rate of increase in human population change.

Year	Human Population
10,000	5–10 million
1 AD	170 million
1800	1 billion
1930	2 billion
1960	3 billion
1975	4 billon
1987	5 billion
1999	6 billion
2012	7 billion
2025	8 billion

United States Census Bureau. "World Population Trends." http://www.census.gov/ipc/www/idb/worldpopinfo.php. Last modified September 10, 2009.

Discuss: What pattern do you notice in the rate of increase? How does this increase affect wild animals and plants? What do you predict the population will be in 2030?

Saving Endangered Species

To save endangered species, we need knowledge. This begins with understanding how endangered species live. Scientists learn about animals by watching their behavior in the wild and studying their habits. While it is unlikely that students will have the chance to observe an endangered species in school or at home, they can learn the skills scientists use in order to help them better understand how people learn to save endangered species. Only with the knowledge scientists gather can they develop plans for helping endangered species recover. With this knowledge, scientists can make a difference.

Watching the School's Wild Animals

Materials: clipboards

Procedure:
Tell your students that they are going to be observing wild animals. Remind them that to observe animals, they have to interfere as little as possible in order not to change the animal's behavior. Scientists need to record their observations so they can remember what they learn, but they also don't want to be so focused on the writing that they are not observing what is going on. This means taking quick notes in words or phrases. Later, after the observations are done, more details can be added.

With clipboard, paper, and pen in hand, the students are off to observe wild animals. Schoolyard wildlife such as squirrels, birds, and insects or even worms can be subjects of study.

Another interesting way to teach this lesson is by using other students. Take your students out to watch another class at recess or during physical education time. These are good situations to observe since there is more action than watching a math class. Your students should sit on the side without disturbing the "wildlife," then observe and take notes. Each of your students should pick one other student on whom to focus.

After they have finished, have the students share their observations. Have them stick to just the facts before they share any theories. No matter what animal they observed, have them imagine the animal has become very rare.

Discuss: Were there any observations you made that would help you to take care of the animals? What questions do you have that would help you to understand the animals better?

Success Stories

Materials: research resources

Procedure:
Because of the hard work of concerned citizens, there are many examples of endangered species that have regained their population so they are no longer on the brink of extinction—some are no longer even endangered. To celebrate this work, students can write newspaper articles to report the good news. As so much of the information that children hear about the environment is focused on problems, it is good for them to learn about the times humans have taken action to help make a positive difference.

The story of the osprey is a good example of how humans can both cause a problem and find solutions that work. Ospreys are fish-eating raptors that live along rivers, lakes, and oceans. They make spectacular dives from high in the air and snatch fish out of the water. Until the 1950s, they were a common sight along coastlines and rivers. However, two factors created a problem for them.

Ospreys prefer to nest in the tops of dead trees near water. They build large nests and return year after year. As more people began living along coastlines, this development meant many fewer nesting sites for osprey. Few homeowners wanted a big dead tree on their lawn, blocking their view of the water.

Another change was taking place in the osprey's habitat. New and powerful pesticides were being developed in an effort to control insect pests. One very effective pesticide was DDT. Large amounts of DDT were sprayed over wetlands to kill mosquitoes. DDT would wash into the water, where it was taken in by small fish, which were eaten by bigger fish, which were eaten by bigger fish that were eventually eaten by osprey. As a top predator, ospreys must eat many fish, and DDT would accumulate in their bodies. DDT did not kill the osprey directly but it did affect their reproductive systems so that the eggs laid by females had thin shells. When the osprey sat on the eggs, the shells would crack.

The osprey population declined severely. Fortunately, before they become extinct, some important actions were taken. One step was the construction of nesting platforms. These structures consist of a large, flat platform on top of a telephone pole. Nesting platforms provided the osprey with a place to build their nests that the trees once did.

Another important step was the decision to ban the use of DDT in the United States. Inspired by Rachel Carson's book *Silent Spring*, enough support was generated to stop the use of DDT. Without the DDT in the ecosystem, ospreys were no longer eating fish with DDT. Their population was able to recover to a safe level.

The Center for Biological Diversity has information on 100 examples of success stories due to the Endangered Species Act at http://www.esasuccess.org/reports/.

Students pick an animal to research and write a newspaper article reporting the success story. They will need to answer the following questions:

Who: Describe the animal you are writing about.

What: What happened to the animal?

Where: Where did this take place?

When: When did this all take place?

Why: Why did people cause the animal to become endangered?

How: How did people help the animal or plant recover?

Local Endangered Species

Much of the attention on endangered species is focused on charismatic mega fauna, animals such as pandas, tigers, and whales, and the cute animals or the big ones. These species are animals that often live in faraway places to which the students have very little connection. Unfortunately, there are so many endangered species that each state has its own list. Students can learn about these endangered species and find what they can do to help through their state environmental conservation departments.

The United States Fish and Wildlife Service has lists of endangered species for each state at http://ecos.fws.gov/tess_public/pub/stateListingAndOccurrence.jsp.

Protection Posters

Materials: art supplies, posterboards

Procedure:
With words and pictures, students create posters to focus attention on local endangered species. Each poster should present the following information:

Name of endangered species

Drawing of endangered species

Interesting facts
Causes of the problem
How people can help protect the endangered species
Look for places outside of the school where the posters can be hung up, such as libraries, food stores, etc.

Endangered Species Autobiography

Materials: research resources

Procedure:
Students research an endangered species and write a report as if they were the animals. Instead of students simply reading a book or finding a Web site, they write letters and/or e-mails to get information from a primary source, either from an organization active in the work of saving endangered species or from a scientist whose research is part of an effort to save an endangered species.

After doing some basic research about the animal, provide information such as:
This is what I look like.
This is where I live.
This is what I do.
This is what happened to me.
These basic facts can be the basis for more in-depth questions to the scientist or activist.

The students should send letters that reflect their prior knowledge as well as ask specific questions that follow up on what they have learned through their research. Since it will vary greatly in the response time, you will need to be flexible with deadlines.

Design a Zoo

Zoos are an important part of the efforts to save endangered species from extinction. Many zoos have programs that help endangered species reproduce in captivity with the goal to eventually release the animals into their natural habitat.

Materials: art supplies, research resources

Procedure:
In order for the endangered species to reproduce successfully, its enclosure in the zoo must be as close as possible to the animal's natural habitat. Students should find the answers to as many of the following questions as they can and use this information to create a zoo by designing an enclosure that will lead to the successful reproduction of the animal.
What does the animal eat?
How much water does the animal need?
What temperature does the animal prefer?
What kind of shelter does the animal need?
How big does the enclosure have to be?
What plants and other animals could be used to make the enclosure more natural?
How would you give the animal privacy from human visitors?
What type of floor covering would you use?
What type of lighting would you need?
What should be the humidity of the enclosure?
How will you maintain the enclosure?
Once the students have collected as much information as possible, they use it to either draw or design a model of their enclosure for the animal.

Using the Internet, students can take an online field trip to zoos around the world to get ideas. They can put all their models together and make zoos and give tours to other classes.

The National Zoo in Washington, DC, has an extensive breeding program for endangered species. This Web site has ideas and information for students to use: http://nationalzoo.si.edu/ConservationAnd Science/EndangeredSpecies/CapBreedPops/default.cfm.

Laws to Protect Endangered Species

Materials: government addresses

Procedure:
To better understand how legislation is enacted and enforced, students will use their congressional representatives as information sources. The students can write letters to their representatives to learn more about legislation to protect endangered species.

The Endangered Species Act

The Endangered Species Act of 1973 (ESA) was one of the most important pieces of environmental legislation ever enacted. The purpose of the act is to protect species and also "the ecosystems upon which they depend." The act showed that natural world is of "esthetic, ecological, recreational, and scientific value to our nation and people."

When a population of animals and plants is documented as endangered and/or threatened, it is placed on the endangered species list. Once on the list, the law requires a recovery plan to be developed by the Fish and Wildlife Service. The ESA is credited for saving 99.9 percent of the species that have been listed. Once the population has recovered, the animal or plant can be delisted. The home page for the Endangered Species Act is http://www.fws.gov/endangered/.

Scavenger Hunt at Endangered Species Web Site

Materials: computer, scavenger-hunt sheet

Procedure:
The students will go to the Endangered Species Act page mentioned above and search the site to find the answers to the following questions:

What year was the Endangered Species Act signed into law? 1973

Who was president at the time? Richard Nixon

What does USFWS stand for? United States Fish and Wildlife Service

What region number do you live in?

What is the phone number for the USFWS? 703-358-2061

In the Endangered Species Act, what does recovery mean? The species no longer needs protection.

Name one animal that has been delisted.

What is a HCP? Habitat Conservation Plan.

What are some animals and plants that are being proposed for listing?

Where can you find a list of all the endangered species in the United States? Species Info Link.

What is a Recovery Champion? A Fish and Wildlife staffer whose work is advancing the recovery of an endangered species.

Extension: Students can learn more about CITES, The Convention on International Trade in Endangered Species of Wild Fauna and Flora. This international treaty is designed to regulate the export and import of endangered and threatened species.

Research Resources

1. This Web site from Countdown 2010 has a lot of basic facts and statistics that you and your students can use for their research: http://www.countdown2010.net/?id=171.

2. The Defenders of Wildlife has fact sheets on 50 different endangered species that students can use for their research: http://www.kidsplanet.org/factsheets/map.html.

3. Animalinfo.org has a Web site with information on almost every endangered species and will be a great resource for your students: http://www.animalinfo.org/.

4. The United States of Department of Agriculture has a Web site on endangered plants with an index of species and links to more information: http://plants.usda.gov/threat.html. The Center for Plant Conservation has resources to learn about various endangered plants: http://www.centerforplantconservation. org/NC_Choice.html.

Extinction

Posters

Materials: construction paper, art supplies

Procedure:
Students can create a powerful message by making a poster for animals and plants that have gone extinct due to human actions. On the poster, the students write, "Here lies (name of animal or plant) that became extinct in the year _____ due to _____."

Students can make the posters and put them up on a bulletin board or hang them in public places where more people can learn from them.

References

Kriesberg, Daniel A. *A Sense of Place: Teaching Children about the Environment with Picture Books.* Illustrated by Dorothy Frederick. Englewood, CO: Teacher Ideas Press, 1999. 1-56308-565-8.

"Why Save Endangered Species." United States Fish and Wildlife Service http://www.fws.gov/ endangered/pdfs/Why_Save_End_Species_July_2005.pdf

CHAPTER 4

Resource Depletion

Books

Alter, Anna. *What Can You Do with an Old Red Shoe?* New York: Henry Holt and Company, 2009. 978-0-8050-8290-6.

This is an activity book explaining various ways to recycle common household items into something new. Among the ideas are ways to reuse a shower curtain, a calendar, a blanket, and of course an old red shoe. For each item, there are detailed instructions illustrated by animal characters. Even if students do not make any of the items, the book will give them ideas for ways to reuse other materials. Students can challenge themselves in a contest for the most creative way to reuse a household item.

Atkins, Jeannine. *Aani and the Tree Huggers.* Illustrated by Venantius J. Pinto. New York: Lee and Low Books, Inc., 1995. 1-880000-24-5.

In the 1970s, women in northern India stopped loggers from cutting down the forests around their village by hugging the trees and putting their bodies before the axes. This movement spread to other places and forced village councils to decide how many trees can be cut without harming the long-term sustainability of the forest. *Aani and the Tree Huggers* is based on this story and shows what

can be done if people stand together in the use of nonviolence. The illustrations are painted in traditional Indian styles.

Ayres, Pam. *When Dad Cuts Down the Chestnut Tree*. Illustrated by Graham Percy. New York: Alfred A. Knopf, 1988. 0-394-80435-X.

A short picture book that begins with all the wonderful things Dad can make if he cuts down the chestnut tree and ends with all the things that will be lost if Dad cuts down the chestnut tree. This is a great story for discussing the balance we must seek between using natural resources and conserving them. To better understand the dilemma, students can list all the things in their homes made from wood.

Baylor, Byrd. *The Table Where Rich People Sit*. Illustrated by Peter Parnell. New York: Charles Scribner's Sons, 1994. 0-684-19653-0.

Words and pictures combine beautifully in this book about a family that has a unique way of measuring their wealth. Mountain Girl calls a family meeting to discuss why her parents will not get real jobs and make more money. Instead of counting the value of their material possessions, her parents focus on the experiences and relationships they have in their lives. Mountain Girl begins to realize this is what makes them truly rich. After reading the book, students can create their own lists of what makes them rich.

Ering, Timothy B. *The Story of Frog Belly Rat Bone*. Cambridge, MA: Candlewick Press, 2003. 0-7636-1382-7.

In a grey place of junk and cement, a boy searches for a treasure. He finally finds a box with the note "Put my wondrous riches into the earth and enjoy." He puts the treasures in the ground and also makes a monster out of junk to protect them. The riches grow into a garden of flowers, fruits, and vegetables. Unique illustrations tell this story of recycling and hope.

Gerson, Mary-Joan. *Why the Sky Is Far Away, A Nigerian Folktale*. Illustrated by Carla Golembe. Boston, MA: Little Brown and Company, 1995. 0-316-30852-8.

Back in the time when people did not have to grow crops, they simply reached into the sky for food. It was simple and easy, but after a time, the people began to waste more and more. The sky became angry and told the people to waste no more. They tried but could not stop, so the sky sailed out of reach and the people were forced to farm the land. The story is a good example of how people long ago taught children how to live. Even today there is much that can be learned from this Nigerian folktale.

Goodman, Susan E. *Nature Did It First!* Photographs by Dorothy Handelman. Brookfield, CT: The Millbrook Press, 2003. 0-7613-2413-5.

This book is a good introduction to biomimicry, the design technique using nature's model to solve problems and invent new products. By modeling nature's designs, humans can work within the limits of ecology. The book matches a human invention with an example of how nature did it first. For example, we have straws and butterflies that have a hollow tongue to suck up nectar from a flower. We have helmets and other protective gear and armadillos that have bones in their skin for armor. This book can inspire students to look for more examples of biomimicry and new ways to use nature for ideas.

Inches, Alison. *The Adventures of a Plastic Bottle*. Illustrated by Pete Whitehead. New York: Little Green Books, 2009. 1416967885.

The plastic water bottle tells his adventures in the form of a diary as he goes from being underground to a refinery, to a manufacturing plant, to a store shelf, and finally to being recycled into a fleece jacket. While is good for students to see how plastic is recycled, they should also understand that most plastic water bottles are simply thrown away. Students can find out where the water bottles they use come from and where they go.

Jeffers, Oliver. *The Great Paper Caper*. New York: Philomel Books, 2008. 0007182333.

Someone is cutting down the trees and the forest creatures cannot figure out who, so they set out to solve the mystery. Their detective work leads them to Bear. He is cutting down the trees so he can make more paper to win a paper-airplane contest. At his trial, Bear promises to plant new trees and protect the old ones. The other animals collect old paper airplanes so that Bear can reuse them. It is a funny story with whimsical drawings.

Kusugak, Michael. *Who Wants Rocks?* Illustrated by Vladyana Langer Krykorka. Toronto: Annick Press, 1999. 1550375881.

Poor Old Joe the prospector comes to Little Mountain to look for gold. When he finds a nugget, he yells "gold" and all the other prospectors come rushing over and chop away at the mountain, taking more and more away. Poor Old Joe watches the mountains being destroyed and feels sad, so he tricks the other prospectors by yelling "rocks!" The prospectors stop rushing over. Joe learns the true riches are the beauty of the mountains.

Lish, Ted. *It's Not My Job*. Illustrated by Charles Jordan. Victorville, Alberta: Munchweiler Press, 2002. 0-7940-0004-5.

This is the humorous story of a family that does not take out the trash in their new home because everyone says, "It is not my job." When the trash completely fills the house, everyone in the family finally realizes that they are all responsible for taking out the trash. Students can discuss how this story of one family translates to the garbage crisis in our world.

Lorbiecki, Marybeth. *Paul Bunyan's Sweetheart*. Illustrated by Renee Graef. Chelsea, MI: Sleeping Bear Press, 2007. 978-1-58536-289-9.

This is an interesting take on the legend of Paul Bunyan. He falls in love with Lucette, who is so big her quilt becomes farm fields, and when she shakes out her rug, it causes a tornado. Before Lucette would marry Paul, she gave him some tests, which he failed. He did not win her heart until he listened to her about caring for the forest, instead of just cutting the trees. Paul and his lumberjacks replanted a tree for each one they cut down, and now there will be a wedding.

Page, Linda Glaser. *Compost?* Brookfield, CT: Millbrook Press, 1996. 0761300309

A good introduction to how one family uses a compost pile to recycle their garbage and garden waste. The book is brightly illustrated and there is some additional information on the back pages and experiments students can try. Even a small compost bucket will show the students how the compost process works.

Porcellino, John. *Thoreau at Walden*. New York: Hyperion, 2008. 978-1-4231-0038-6.

Using the words of Henry David Thoreau and a graphic novel format, this book tells the story of his time at Walden Pond. Thoreau's words speak to the simplicity and wisdom he believed were necessary for a life well-lived. A discussion of Thoreau's writing in this book will inspire conversations and thoughts about how to live with less. The words written at Walden inspired countless others to live a life closer to the natural world.

Portis, Antoinette. *Not a Box*. New York: HarperCollins, 2006. 0061112321.

This cute and simple book reminds us how far a cardboard box and an imagination can take a child. The author uses a simply drawn rabbit to show the reader some of the many things a box can be. The book has a subtle environmental message about using fewer material goods and recycling what we do have.

Shannon, David. *Too Many Toys*. New York: Blue Sky Press, 2008. 10:0-439-49029-4.

This is a fun story with big color illustrations about a boy named Spencer who has enough toys to fill his house. Finally, his mother tells him he needs to get rid of some of the toys he does not play with anymore. After they pack them all up in a big box, they take a break to rest. Spencer's mom returns and sees that he has dumped all the toys back out. He is still ready to get rid of the toys but he wants the box because, "it's the best toy ever." A great take on overconsumption and the fun a child can have with only a box, some recycled materials, and an imagination.

Slavin, Bill. *Transformed: How Everyday Things are Made*. Tonawanda, NY: Kids Can Press, 2007. 1554532442.

This is a great resource to teach students about the life cycle of 69 everyday products. The text explains the step-by-step process that goes into making items such as bricks, toothpaste, erasers and more. Each item has a two-page spread that includes illustrations and interesting historical facts. As the students learn about the life cycle of these products, they can look for ways to make the products more environmentally sustainable.

Strauss, Rochelle. *One Well: The Story of Water on the Earth*. Illustrated by Rosemary Woods. Tonawanda, NY: Kids Can Press, 2007. 978-1-55337-9546.

When people think of all the water on the Earth coming from one well, people will care for that water as their own. This book gets the message across by explaining how water is used by plants, animals, and people, combined with sidebars of interesting facts on every page. The book also includes background information for teachers and parents to help further explain the concepts in the book and provides ideas for taking action. We all share one well of water.

Thompson, Colin. *The Paper Bag Prince*. New York: Alfred A Knopf, Inc., 1992. 0-679-83048-0.

There is a dump near a town where more and more garbage is piling up and up. Despite the trash, there are a few animals and plants waiting for the chance to grow and blossom again. The Paper Bag Prince comes to visit each day, and when the dump closes, he moves in and lives there, both watching the life return and helping make it happen. The intricate illustrations show the reader how much life there is in a dump.

Activities

To make all the products we use and enjoy, a lot of natural resources are needed. Producing the cars, toys, electronics, books, furniture, and all the rest takes tremendous amounts of water, minerals, wood, oil, and other raw materials. These materials come from underground, from the water, and from the forests. Extracting these resources causes environmental problems, processing these raw materials causes environmental problems, disposing of these materials causes environmental problems, and in addition, many of these resources are non-renewable, which means we are going to run out of them if we are not careful.

Primarily, we use resources in a linear fashion. We get them from the Earth, make them into something, sell them, buy them, and throw them away where they cannot be used again. If the linear system is changed to one in which materials are not simply thrown away to a system where we reduce, reuse, recycle, and repair, then it becomes a renewable cycle with much less pollution and that is more sustainable. This chapter will focus on how we obtain and use materials as well as how we can reduce the amount of materials we use. The effects of using these materials on the environment will be covered in the next chapter.

Using Resources

Many of the raw materials needed to make the products we use come from underground. To obtain these materials, we must dig or drill into the earth. This simulation will begin a discussion about how this process is done and what is left behind.

Mining Chocolate Chips

Materials: chocolate chip cookies, toothpicks

Procedure:
The cookies represent the earth, the chocolate chips represent the raw materials we need, and the toothpicks are the tools and machines we use to obtain the raw materials.

Give each student a cookie and a toothpick. Without any introduction, tell them that their goal is to get the chips out of the cookies using only the toothpick. Observe the different techniques the students use to dig out the chips. Some will quickly break up the cookies into crumbs and take out the chocolate chips; other will slowly chip away without breaking up the cookies very much. Remind them not to eat any cookies yet. After five to ten minutes, stop the work and tell them to put the cookie back together without the chips. After a pause to listen to their comments, tell them what the cookies and chips represent. Discuss:

Can the cookie be put together? Why is it difficult?

How is this activity like mining and drilling for oil?

What are the environmental impacts of mining?

What happens to the leftover materials that were not used for manufacturing?

Is there a technique to get the chips that will cause less damage to the cookie?

How would this apply to real mining?

Which techniques will cost more in the short run?

Which techniques will cost more in the long run?

Do you think people will be willing to pay more for products that were produced from raw materials that were obtained in a more environmentally sensitive manner?

What happens if we use up all the chips and there are no more cookies?

What happens if we use fewer chips?

Vocabulary:

Ore: Rocks that contain mineral used to manufacture products.

Tailings: Leftover, unusable materials when processing the ores into usable materials.

Reclamation: Actions taken to reclaim the land and attempt to restore the habitat that was affected by the mining or drilling.

Extensions:
Give out another cookie and have a contest to see who can get out the chips while causing the least amount of damage to the earth.

Eat the cookies!

How Much Do We Take?

Materials: estimating sheet

Procedure:
Students fill in the sentences to estimate the amount of materials used per capita from mining each year.

Name:

Fill in the blanks with the number of pounds you estimated are used to make the following items.

1. Every year we use _____ pounds of cement to build roads, bridges, buildings, etc.

2. Every year we use _____ pounds of iron ore to make all the steel we use.

3. Every year we use _____ pounds of aluminum for beverage containers, airplanes, and other products.

4. Every year we use _____ pounds of zinc to make metals, paints, etc.

5. Every year we use _____ pounds of copper to make electrical parts.

6. Every year we use _____ pounds of clay to make floors, tiles, and kitty litter.

7. Every year we use _____ pounds of coal.

Answer Key

1. 714 pounds of cement to build roads, bridges, buildings, etc.

2. 377 pounds of iron ore to make all the steel we use.

3. 84 pounds of aluminum for beverage containers, airplanes, and other products.

4. 7 pounds of zinc to make metals, paints, etc.

5. 15 pounds of copper to make electrical parts.

6. 204 pounds of clay to make floors, tiles, and kitty litter.

7. 7,378 pounds of coal.

Mineral Mining Institute. "Per Capita Use of Minerals in the United States," mii.org, 2009.

Water/No Water

Water is a resource we need for everything.

Materials: two coffee cans, index cards

Procedure:
To prepare the game, use two sets of coffee cans. Label one "water" and one "no water." On each index card, write the name of various animals, plants, and animate and inanimate objects, such as dog, cat, rock, ice cream, tulip, table, car, etc. Divide the students into two teams, arranged in a line. Put the can about 20 yards away from the lines. Indoors, the students can walk through the game. This is a relay race; the first person in line will hand out the cards. The students run down and decide which can to put the card in. If they think the item on the card needs water, they put it in the "water" can; if not, it goes into the "no water" can. The winning team is the one that finishes first, but the team loses time for a card that is in the wrong can.

After the race, bring the cans back and go through the cards to see if they are in the correct place. Start with the water bucket and pull one card out a time. Ask the class if they think the card is in the right place. Any card in the "water" bucket is correct. Go to the other team and talk through the cards in their "water" can. Next, go through the "no water" can. As you pull out each card, ask the group if they think it is in the right place. Everything needs water at some point in its existence. For example, the table is made from wood from a tree, and the tree needed water. The car needs water in its radiator; the cup needs water to process the plastic. Any card in the "no water" bucket is automatically wrong, so if they say "no," lead them through the connections.

Guess the Amount of Water

Materials: estimating sheet

Procedure:
Ask the students to estimate how much water it takes to produce certain items. Then give them the answer to see if they become better at estimating how much water it takes to produce these items.

Name:

How Much Water Does It Take to Make:

1. One pound of plastic
2. A new car
3. Cotton T-shirt
4. One watermelon
5. One loaf of bread
6. One egg
7. One chicken
8. One pound of plastic
9. One ton of steel
10. One gallon of paint
11. One can of fruit

Did you get better at your estimates?

What surprised you the most?

Pick another item in your house. How much water does it take to make?

Answer Key

One pound of plastic	24 gallons
A new car	39,090 gallons
Cotton T-shirt	400 gallons
One watermelon	100 gallons
One loaf of bread	150 gallons
One egg	120 gallons
One chicken	400 gallons
One pound of plastic	24 gallons
One ton of steel	62,600 gallons
One gallon of paint	13 gallons
One can of fruit	9.3 gallons

Charlotte Harbor National Estuary Program. "Water Conservation Facts." March 27, 2006. http://www.chnep.org/MoreInfo/water_conservation_facts.htm.

How Many Trees Does It Take to Build a House?

So much of what we use is made from wood, but do we really have any sense of how many trees it takes to make all these things? To find out how much usable wood is in a tree, foresters need two measurements: the height of the tree and the area of the tree. Foresters use board feet to measure the amount of usable wood in a tree. One board foot is equal to a piece of wood that is one foot by one foot by one inch. To show children how many trees it takes to build a house, go outside and measure a tree in the schoolyard. Pick the biggest tree you can find.

Materials: yardsticks, string, calculator

Procedure:

Step one:
Measure the height of the tree using one of the following methods. Measure the height up to the point in the tree where the trunk ends and the tree branches out.

Student size method:
Stand a student of known height next to the tree, using the student as a benchmark for the rest of the class to estimate the size of the tree. For example, if Jill is five feet tall and stands next to the tree, how many Jills tall is the tree?

Ruler method:
A student holds a ruler in his or her hand and walks away from the tree. At about fifty yards, the student holds the ruler out in front and lines up the tree with the top of their fist at the bottom of the tree and the top of the ruler in line with the point where the tree branches out from the trunk. Next, turn the ruler sideways, keeping the top of the fist in line with the bottom of the tree. Another student walks out from the base of the tree until they are standing in line with the end of the ruler. A third student measures the distance from the base of the tree to the spot where the second student is standing. That distance is the height of the tree.

Step two:
The next measurement you need is the area; to figure this out, you need the circumference of the tree at 4 and 1/2 feet off the ground. If you do not have a tape measure, you can use a piece of string and then lay it against a yardstick.

How Many Trees Are in Your House?

You will need to do the following calculations:

1. To figure out the area divide the circumference by 3.14 (pi) to get the diameter.
2. Divide the diameter by 2 to get the radius.
3. Divide the radius by 12 to convert inches to feet.
4. The formula to find the area of a circle is A = r^2 x pi (3.14). (Area = radius squared times 3.14).
5. To find the volume in cubic board feet, multiply the area (feet) x height (feet) / 4 (foresters divide by 4 to account for the taper of the tree).
6. Since 12 board feet of lumber equals 1 cubic foot, multiply cubic board feet by 12 to find the volume in board feet.

Tree species: _____

1. Height _____ feet.
2. Circumference _____ inches.
3. Circumference divided by 3.14 equals diameter _____ inches.
4. Diameter divided by two equals radius _____ inches.
5. Divide radius by 12 to convert to feet _____ feet.
6. Radius squared times 3.14 equals area _____ square inches.
7. Area times height equals volume of tree in cubic feet = above number times tree height / 4 = _____.
8. Volume of tree in board feet = above number times 12 = _____.

Step three:

A small ranch-style house with three bedrooms is about 1,000 square feet; this would take about 3,000 board feet of lumber to build. Have students estimate the number of trees that would be needed to build the house they live in.

Extensions:

Students measure trees on their own to find out which tree would provide the most feet for building.

Research how many sheets of paper could come from their tree.

Discuss ways we can use less wood.

This activity was adapted from the United States Forest Service. United States Department of Agriculture, Forest Service, Northeast Region. "Calculating Board Footage in a Tree." http://www.na.fs. fed.us/spfo/pubs/uf/lab_exercises/calc_board_footage.htm.

Using Paper

To understand the effectiveness of conservation efforts, we need to know where we started. To evaluate the work being done to conserve resources, you have to know where you are starting to know if you are getting there. For example, in order to know if efforts to conserve paper are working, students need to know how much paper is actually being used.

Materials: Calculators

Procedure:

Find out how many sheets of paper your school uses each month. Using various educational and awareness tactics, begin a paper conservation effort at school. There could be a contest for the most creative ways to reuse a sheet of paper. For greater impact, students can express the amount of paper in the numbers of miles the paper would stretch if lined up end to end. As you work on efforts to use less paper, ask the school's business office to track how much paper is being ordered. Publicize the results as a way to motivate the school community. Graphs can be used to track the improvements.

How Much Is Left Over?

Students can get a sense of how much garbage is thrown away by weighing and analyzing it in their classroom and at home.

Materials: scale, recording sheet

Procedure:

For one week, have students measure how much garbage is thrown away. They record the results and find the average per day for the class. To take this to the next step, students can sort the garbage to find out specifically how much plastic, paper, metal, and food is being thrown away.

Discuss:

What does it mean for the environment to throw so much material away?

What if the garbage became the raw materials for new products instead of having to take new raw materials from the Earth?

What do you think landfill-mining means?

Extensions:
Students look into garbage cans around the school and record what they find. They do not need to pick through the cans, just take a peek inside. From these observations and the data collected, students can classify the materials that are thrown away and think of ways to reduce the wasted materials.

Who Needs Soil?

Soil is an essential resource. Nearly all of our food is dependant on soil. Either we eat plants that grow in the soil or we eat animals that ate plants grown in soil.

Materials: chart paper

Procedure:
To show students this, have them pick a favorite food, for example, pizza. Ask them: What do we need to make a pizza? Cheese.

What do we need to make cheese? Cows.

What do we need to have cows? Grass.

What do we need to have grass? Soil.

Even fish are affected by the minerals and soil that erode into the water.

The students can pick another favorite food and make their own charts.

From *Think Green, Take Action: Books and Activities for kids* by Daniel A. Kriesberg. Santa Barbara, CA: Libraries Unlimited. Copyright © 2010.

Racing for Soil

If we need soil for so much, it is important to know the soil's ingredients. The main ingredients of soil are:

Dead organic matter (provides nutrients)

Rocks (provide minerals)

Water

Air

Live plants (to help prevent erosion and as a source of dead organic matter)

Decomposers (bacteria, fungi, and animals that help break down the dead organic materials)

Materials: trays

Procedure:
Take your students outside and divide them into groups of three or four. Tell them it is a race to find the six ingredients of soil: decomposers, rocks, dead organic materials, air, water, and live plants. The students run off and put the ingredients in the tray. When they think they are done, they should come back to you. Look through the trays with the students and check off what they have and do not have. If they are missing something, send them back to figure it out. Most likely, they will not think of water and air as ingredients of soil. They do not have to bring back water and air; all they have to do is tell you. The last ingredient is the "time" it takes to make soil. To dramatize this, drop a watch into the tray and say "100 to 400 years." Understanding this concept teaches us the value of soil as well as the extent of the problem when soil is eroded away or misused.

Erosion, Weathering, and Soil

Now that the students know the importance of soil and what it is made from, they can learn more about what is happening to it. Erosion is the movement of soil from one place to another. Sometimes erosion can deposit soil in places that benefits people by providing soil that can be used for farming. Most often soil is eroded away and washed into rivers, lakes, and oceans, where it is lost to the land. Erosion is a natural process but human actions have increased the amount of erosion and its impact on ecosystems.

Materials: water, wood boards

Procedure:
Take the students outside to look for examples of erosion around the school. Check for places where water flows, wind blows, or where people are creating paths by walking over grass instead of on the sidewalk. To help them better understand erosion, try this activity. If there is a place where students can make a pile of dirt, let them build a mountain. Once the mountains are built, have them blow on the mountains to demonstrate wind erosion. Then sprinkle water on top to demonstrate water erosion from rain. Pour water on top to demonstrate erosion from rivers. Splash the sides with water to demonstrate wave erosion.

There are two major factors that affect the amount of erosion that takes place. One is the slope of the land. The steeper the land, the faster the water moves over it, thereby carrying away more soil. To demonstrate this, place soil on a board. Pour water on the top of the board and have the students observe how much soil is eroded way. Hold another board at an angle and pour the same amount of water over the top of this board. Compare the amounts of soil that erodes away. If you can find a place in the schoolyard with a slope, demonstrate the difference between erosion on a slope versus erosion on flat ground.

Another important factor rate of erosion is the amount of plants growing on the land. If you have a place around your school with a slope and no ground cover, you can pour water on the ground to compare that to a place with ground cover. In some places, you may be able to pull up some grass to demonstrate deforestation. Pour water down the slope and observe which slope has more erosion. Discuss how the plant roots help to hold the soil in place. This means that deforestation is followed by erosion. This erosion can lead to the loss of farmland; it makes it harder for forests to regenerate. In addition, lakes and rivers become silted up with soil.

Food Waste

When food is wasted, it is not just the meal that is being thrown out. It is also all the resources that went into making the food.

Materials: scale

Procedure:
In cooperation with the school cafeteria, come up with a procedure that will allow your students to measure food waste. Perhaps there can be a separate garbage receptacle for food waste only. Then at the end of the meal, students weigh the leftovers.

If you cannot have your students do this at school, they can weigh food waste at home.
Once they have gathered the data, students should graph the results in order to look for patterns and draw conclusions for ways to waste less food. Students can also survey grocery stores and restaurants about how much food is wasted.

They can test their creativity by coming up with ways to have a waste-free lunch. This would require some parent education, but with some awareness and effort, students can figure out ways to recycle, reduce, and reuse materials so that they can have a waste-free lunch.

Renewable Versus Non-renewable

Materials: survey sheet, candies, jar

Procedure:
Students create a survey sheet to list items they find around the school and check them off if they are made from a renewable resource or a non-renewable one. Have them compare lists for patterns and similarities. An interesting way to demonstrate the difference between these two types of resources is to use candy as a model. Only about 7 percent of the fuel we use comes from renewable resources. Take 100 candies and mark seven of them with a circle; the marked candies represent renewable energy resources such as hydropower, solar energy, wind energy, and geothermal. Students take one candy out of a jar and eat it. If it was marked as renewable, put another candy back in to replace it. If it was non-renewable, do not put any candy back in the jar. Give more students a chance to pick a candy. Discuss what is happening to the non-renewable energy sources. What would happen if we put in more candy that was marked as renewable energy? Would the game last longer?

Energy Information Administration. "Energy in Brief." http://tonto.eia.doe.gov/energy_in_brief/ renewable_energy.cfm.

Where Does Your Water Come From?

Since water is an essential resource, it is important students and all of us know where it comes from in order to be able to keep it clean.

Materials: none

Procedure:
Start with the water fountain or sink in the classroom. Talk to a custodian to find out where the pipes lead from the sink. Perhaps he can take the students on a trip to the basement to show them where the pipes lead out of the school. Speak with someone from the local water district to find out the source of water for your community. It is important to know and understand where your community gets its drinking water. Where the water comes from influences how your community should be caring for the land. If the drinking water comes from underground in an aquifer, then good decisions must be made about caring for the land above the aquifer. If your community gets its water from a lake, river, or reservoir, then good decisions must be made about caring for the land surrounding the water and the water itself.

You can go to the Environmental Protection Agency's Web site for Local Drinking Water Information and get drinking water reports for your community: http://www.epa.gov/safewater/dwinfo/ index.html.

If your community gets its water from a lake, river, or reservoir, have students find the source of water on a map. Figure out how far the water travels to get to your home or school.

If your community gets its water from an aquifer, here is a simple model to show students. Explain to them that an aquifer is an area under the earth's surface made of rocks and sand that water can easily move through and stay between the spaces. Fill a clear container about three-quarters of the way to the top with sand, gravel, and rocks. Pour enough water into the container to fill in the empty spaces. Do not pour so much water into the container that water covers all the rocks; the top of the rocks should be dry. The base of the cup acts as a barrier from the water draining out. In a real aquifer, bedrock or clay holds the water in place. You can use a straw to model how water is pumped out of an aquifer.

Discuss:

What happens if too much water is pumped out? (The aquifer will drain.)

How does new water recharge the aquifer? (Rain, snow)

What can happen to prevent water from recharging the aquifer? (Roads, buildings, and other developments prevent water from sinking into the ground.)

How do we prevent pollution from getting into the aquifer? (By being very careful about what we put in the ground above the aquifer.)

Energy Audit

Since so much energy is used to heat and cool our homes, conserving some of this energy has many environmental benefits. Plus, by saving energy, each homeowner is also saving money. A building that is not energy-efficient is heating and cooling the outdoors.

Materials: energy audit sheet, pencil, tape, plastic wrap

Procedure:
Here are some simple ways students can audit their home or school to find out how much energy is being wasted. Give each student a copy of the audit sheet to take home. They can also use the draft detector to look for places where air is going in and out of the house.

Tape the top edge of a 6-inch by 6-inch sheet of plastic wrap so that the rest of the plastic hangs down. Hold the draft detector in front of places where air may be coming into the building. The students use the following checklist to audit the building.

Home Energy Audit

Name:

Are walls and cciling light enough in color to reflect heat?	Yes	No
If there is a fireplace, does it have damper and glass doors?	Yes	No
On windy days, do the draft detectors show air movement through electrical outlets on outside walls?	Yes	No
Are there any other places where the draft detector shows air?	Yes	No
Movement?	Yes	No
Are hot water facets dripping?	Yes	No
If there are baseboard radiators, are they free of dust?	Yes	No
Has the furnace been cleaned in the last year?	Yes	No
Are there evergreen shrubs or trees on the north side of the house to block wind?	Yes	No
Are there any air leaks between the house and foundation or air leaks in the basement?	Yes	No
Are lights and other electrical appliances left on when not in use?	Ycs	No
Is the thermostat kept higher than 62 degrees?	Yes	No
Have lighthulbs been switched to compact florescent lightbulbs?	Yes	No
Are the walls in the house insulated?	Yes	No
Are clothes sometimes hung to dry instead of put in the dryer?	Yes	No
How would you rate the energy efficiency of the building?		

Plastics Journal

To make students aware of how much plastic they use in their daily lives, have them keep a plastics journal for a week.

Materials: data sheet

Procedure:
Students can use the following data-collection sheet to record their use of plastic.

My Plastic Journal

Name:

Plastic used: _____

Date: _____

How many times was it used before being thrown away? _____

Plastic used: _____

Date: _____

How many times was it used before being thrown away? _____

Plastic used: _____

Date: _____

How many times was it used before being thrown away? _____

Plastic used: _____

Date: ___

How many times was it used before being thrown away? _____

Plastic used: _____

Date: _____

How many times was it used before being thrown away? _____

A Biography of a Cell Phone

The everyday items we use come to us from a widespread web of materials from all over the world. These items are dependant on many resources. To understand the resources that go into these everyday items, we must learn about the life cycles of the products we use.

Materials: research resources

Procedure:

Students should pick a common everyday item to study or the entire class can focus on one example and divide up the research. For each product, there are questions the students should answer to understand its entire life cycle. Encourage them to be creative about writing the biography and presenting the information.

Birth of a cell phone. (What raw materials are used to make a cell phone?)

Where was the cell phone born? (Where do the raw materials come from?)

How does the cell phone grow? (How is the cell phone made?)

What does the cell phone do for a job? (How do people use the cell phone?)

What happens to the cell phone when it dies? (How is a cell phone disposed?)

A poster on the life cycle of a cell phone available from the Environmental Protection Agency can help with the research and serve as a model: http://www.epa.gov/waste/education/pdfs/life-cell.pdf.

Saving Resources: Design Challenges

One of the ways to conserve resources is to design products that use fewer materials, require less energy to operate, and are easier to recycle. An example is cars that are lighter but retain the strength of a heavier car, thereby using less gas. Or a television with separate parts so that if something is wrong, you can just buy a new part instead of a new television. Just by looking around the classroom the students can think of ways to improve the products they use to make them more environmentally sustainable. In the past, products were primarily designed based on appearance, price, and quality. A new parameter is to consider the product's impact on the environment in the design. Keeping the earth in mind does create limits but does not mean that the product cannot still look good, work well, and have a reasonable price. These design challenges ask the students to design a product that meets certain criteria that put limits on what can be done. Just as working with the environment instead of against the environment puts limits on what can be done. The goal of the challenges is not necessarily to design a more sustainable product. The goal is to challenge the students to work within limits. The challenges get them to think about how products are invented, reinvented, and redesigned in order to have less impact on the environment. These challenges inspire the creativity we need to work within the limits of environmental sustainability.

Put the students in groups of two or three and present the challenge. Then, depending on your schedule, give them at least a half hour or more to experiment with their designs and try different ideas. They should have the opportunity to see what works and what doesn't work. For all the challenges, give the students time to experiment, try ideas, and learn from each other. Then hold a contest so they can compare their work with their classmates. During the contest, give everyone two or three chances. If a group uses up all its materials trying one idea, it can resupply to try a new idea. However, make students aware that while it is okay to resupply, they should reuse what they can. Try to set a good example of conserving resources by using recycled materials whenever possible for the challenges.

These design challenges all lead to interesting discussions. After completing the challenges, here are some questions to discuss:

What did you try that worked?

What did you try that did not work?

What did you learn from failing?

What would you try if you had more time?

How did it help to work together?

Was it difficult to work together?

What ideas can we generate from the design challenges that would make insulation, cars, bridges, buildings, and cooking more environmentally sustainable?

What ideas can we develop to redesign common household items to make them more environmentally sustainable?

Extension: What are some of the designs being developed in the real world to make these products less wasteful of resources?

Insulating Ice Cubes

Better insulation can keep our homes warmer in the winter and cooler in the summer while using less energy.

Challenge: Who can make a package using the available materials that will keep an ice cube from melting the least in one hour?

Materials: cups, various materials that can be used to insulate the cups

Rules: Use the cup and the other materials to make a container for the ice cube. In one hour, check the ice cube and measure how much of it has melted. Leave one ice cube in a bowl as a control to see how much difference the packaging makes.

Terrific Towers

Buildings use large amounts of raw materials and require huge amounts of electricity and gas to heat and cool. If we can design buildings to be more energy efficient, a large amount of resources can be saved.

Materials: hair dryer, newspapers, tape

Challenge: Who can build the tallest tower that can stand up to the wind blowing from a hair dryer for 10 seconds from one yard away without falling over?

Rules: You can only use three sheets of newspaper and one yard of masking tape to build the tower.

Note: Place the tower on a table against a wall with an outlet. Hold the blow dryer one yard away and turn on the dryer for 10 seconds. Can the tower remain standing?

Better Bridges

Roads and bridges use vast amounts of materials. If we could build roads with recycled materials, it would take a great deal of resources out of the waste stream.

Materials: paper, small books, batteries or some other objects that can be used as weights

Challenge: Who can build a bridge between two desks that holds the most weight? Rules: You can use only two sheets of paper. The desks must be seven inches apart. The weights cannot be placed over the desks; they must be fully supported by the bridge.

Cooler Cars

Cars place a huge demand on the planet's resources. They use gas and emit carbon dioxide and other pollutants. If we can develop cars that are more efficient, we will save resources, conserve energy, and produce fewer pollutants.

Challenge: Who can make a paper plate car roll the furthest?

Materials: straws, paper plates, tape, ramp

Rules: You can use only four plates, one straw, and one yard of tape. You cannot push the car down the ramp, just let go and let it roll.

<u>Product Packaging</u>

Introduction: One tremendous use of resources is packaging for the products we buy. Very little of this packaging is reused or recycled; most of it is thrown away.

Materials: envelope, packing materials

Challenge: Can you send a single potato chip through the mail from your house to the school without cracking the chip in a package that weighs less then 45 grams?

Rules: If more than one package is successful, the package with the least amount of mass is the winner.

Note: This challenge is best done as homework assignment. The following is a letter you can use with your students.

Name:

Problem:

Today's inventions should take into account their impact on the environment. I make jewelry that is very fragile. I want to be able to send my products to my customers using as little plastic, paper, and other resources as possible. Your challenge is to design a package I can use to ship my jewelry. To test your invention, you must send a single potato chip in the mail with as little damage as possible and in a package with the least amount of mass. On the back of this sheet, you must write a description of what you did to protect your chip.

Materials: one plain potato chip, one envelope addressed to me at school, packaging materials

Rules:

1. Only one potato chip.
2. Chips may not be tampered with at all.
3. Envelopes may not be altered; you cannot write "fragile" on the envelope.
4. The envelope must go through the United States Postal Service.
5. The instructions must be in the envelope.
6. The description must be on the back of the instruction sheet.
7. The envelope must arrive by a certain date to avoid penalty.
8. The group name must be on the outside of the envelope.
9. Parent or guardian's signature required.
10. Put a smiley face on the top of the instructions.

Judging:

The mass of the envelope and the contents will be examined in school. The winner is the student with the least mass and the least number of penalty points.

Bonus Points:

If the chip has no cracks, the student gets 10 points, and 10 points if the envelope's mass is less than 45 grams and the chip is not broken.

<u>Super Solar Cooking</u>
Instead of burning wood or using other fuels for cooking, cooking food directly from the sun will save energy and resources.

Challenge: Who can use the available materials to create the highest temperature?

Materials: thermometer, foil, plates, paper, wire, and other materials

Rules: In case of a tie, the solar oven with the fewest materials wins. The temperature of the oven must be higher than the surface temperature.

Solar Power Experiments

There are many ways we can take advantage of the sun's energy with simple changes in the way we design and construct buildings. Passive solar is the term used to describe solar energy that works without any mechanical means. These experiments will show students how we can use the power of the sun to conserve energy resources.

These are just some suggestions for designing the experiments. Depending on the age and experience of your students, you can adjust how much of the experimental design they will develop themselves and how much will you lay out for them. For older students, simply give them the questions and let them design their own experiment to find the answers. It is important for students to understand how to design and learn from experiments no matter the area of science they are studying. They should understand that in a well-designed experiment, there is only one variable, and the rest must be controlled. By answering these questions, students will have the information to design a house that uses passive solar energy.

The logistics of conducting these experiments does require some flexibility. The key is to have everything ready to go in order to take advantage of a sunny day. Since the students will be checking their experiments periodically, you will need to have something for them to do in between temperature checks.

<u>What Colors Absorb the Most Heat?</u>

Materials: black, white, red, blue, green construction paper, thermometers

Procedure:
Lay out construction paper on the ground and place a thermometer on each one. Measure the temperature every ten minutes and chart the results.

Variables to control: type of paper, thermometer location, paper location, angle of paper
Why is this important? Black water tanks can sit on the roof and provide hot water using energy to heat water. Parts of the house could be painted black to absorb heat.

<u>Does a Sheet of Black Paper Absorb More Heat When it is on an Angle or Laid Flat?</u>

Materials: black paper, clipboard, thermometers

Procedure:
Put one sheet of paper on each clipboard. Prop one clipboard on an angle. Measure the temperature every ten minutes and chart the results.

Variables to control: type of paper, size of paper, location
Why is this important? Panels and roofs can be put on an angle to absorb more heat.

<u>Which Direction Gets the Most Heat? North, South, East, or West?</u>

Materials: four clipboards, black paper, compass, thermometers

Procedure:
Place a sheet of paper on each clipboard. Prop up the clipboards and face one in each direction. Check periodically and record the temperature for as much of the day as you can.

Variables to control: paper, location, angle of board
Why is this important? Parts of the house facing south should take advantage of the extra sunlight. Parts of the house facing north should be protected from the wind.

What Is the Temperature Difference between a Tray with a Plastic Cover and One without a Plastic Cover?

Materials: two trays, thermometers, plastic wrap

Procedure:
Place one thermometer in each tray. Make a plastic roof on one of the trays. Place the trays outdoors and check the temperature every 10 minutes and chart the results.

Variables to control: tray size, location, length of time spent checking the temperature
Why is this important? A greenhouse can be attached to the main house to generate heat that can be blown into the house.

What Materials Take the Longest to Heat Up and Cool Off?

Materials: four trays, rocks, water, sand, thermometers

Procedure:
Place the four trays in a sunny spot. Place rocks in one tray, water in the next, sand in the third, and leave the last one empty. Stick a thermometer into each tray. Record the temperature every 10 minutes for an hour. Next, put the trays in a shady place or bring them inside. Record the temperature every 10 minutes. What conclusions can you draw from the observations?

Why this is important? Different materials heat up and cool off faster then others. A passive solar technique is to build a wall out of rocks or sand that slowly absorbs heat and then slowly cools off, releasing heat to warm the house. Air heats up quickly but cools off quickly. After sharing and discussing the results, the students design a house incorporating what they learned about passive solar power. They can draw the design or make a 3-D model.

There are other ideas that students may want to incorporate into the houses they design: Plant deciduous trees on the south side of the house; they give shade in the summer and when the leaves fall off, let sun in for the winter. Install a retractable overhang on the south side of the house; it provides shade in the summer and can be retracted to let sun in during the winter.

Other passive solar techniques can be found at the following Web sites:

Oikos, The Green Building Source, has a Web site titled "Basic Ideas in Passive Solar Buildings" that has a lot of helpful information at http://www.oikos.com/library/energy_outlet/passive_solar.html. The United States Department of Energy has a Web site, Energy Efficiency and Renewable Energy that has many ideas for passive solar home design. http://www.energysavers.gov/your_home/designing_remodeling/index.cfm/mytopic=10250

Light and Energy Conservation Tips

Turning off lights when you leave a room and other small actions may not seem like much, but if we multiply a small action by millions, it becomes a big action.

Materials: none

Procedure:
Students research and develop as long a list as possible of ways to conserve energy at school and at home.

Recycling Codes

Since there are so many ways to use plastics, there are many different kinds of plastics. Some plastics are more easily recycled then others. The number codes on the bottoms of plastic containers tell us the kind of plastic and whether or not it can be recycled.

Materials: various kinds of plastic containers

Procedure:

Students bring in a wide variety plastic items from home. Remind them to rinse out any food containers. Make a pile of the plastic and have the students sort the plastic containers by the numbers on the bottom. Discuss what they observe about the properties of the containers in each group.

The numbers on the bottom label the different types of plastic based on what chemicals it is made from and whether it can be recycled.

Numbers 1 and 2 are the most common numbers people can recycle. However, many products need to be made from numbers 3 through 5. Products made from numbers 6 and 7 should be avoided as much as possible.

Containers with number 1 are PETE, polyethylene terephthalate. This plastic was first made as a shatterproof container to replace glass bottles. It is a flexible plastic. Common products that are made from recycled PETE are carpets and polyester fiberfill, and it is incorporated into fabrics.

Containers labeled with number 2 are HDPE, high-density polyethylene. It is used in larger containers like milk and water jugs and colored containers such as liquid detergent and shampoo bottles. It is also found in many children's toys. Most plastic grocery bags are made from number 2. HDPE is easily recycled into other containers. The colored version of HDPE is commonly recycled into plastic lumber.

Number 3 is PVC, polyvinyl chloride. Some of the materials made from number 3 are food packaging, shrink-wrap, plastic food wrap, plumbing pipes, and vinyl siding on houses. It is difficult to recycle.

Materials made from number 4 are LDPE, low-density polyethylene. It is used to make flexible products like bread bags and zip-close food storage bags. It is sometimes recycled into plastic bags and plastic lumber, but it is rarely cost-effective, so most items made from number 4 are thrown into a landfill.

Containers made from number 5 are polypropylene. It is used for reusable food storage containers, yogurt and margarine tubs, syrup bottles, outdoor carpet, and diapers. In most cases, it is still uneconomical to recycle plastic number 5, so both new and old polypropylene products end up in a landfill.

Number 6 plastic is PS, polystyrene. It used to make disposable plastic eating utensils and take-out food containers and materials made from Styrofoam. It is cannot be recycled because it is still cheaper to produce polystyrene from oil than it is to collect and recycle used polystyrene.

Plastic number 7 is made from any combination of any kind of plastic. The caps and lids of recyclable bottles are usually made from number 7. Plastic number 7 cannot be recycled; when given a choice, do not buy materials made from this plastic.

University of Missouri, School of Polymer Science. "What Do Those Recycling Numbers Mean?" http://pslc.ws/macrog//work/recycle.htm.

The Daily Green. "What Do Recycling Symbols on Plastic Mean?" by Brian Howard Clark. http://www.thedailygreen.com/green-homes/latest/recycling-symbols-plastics-460321.

Changing Behavior: Needs Versus Wants

In this day and age, it is easy for people to think that something they want is really something they need. It is this line of thinking that leads to overconsumption that leads to resource depletion.

Materials: none

Procedure:
To increase their understanding of necessities versus luxuries, have the students write two lists. One would include items that are necessary for living and the other items that are luxuries. Discuss which list is longer. Does everyone agree with what are luxuries and necessities? Where do the resources come from to produce the items? Are there alternatives to these items that use fewer resources? How does owning so many luxuries affect the environment? The purpose of this activity is not to make the children feel guilty for having these products. The purpose is to empower them by understanding that they have choices.

Back in the Day

To find out how attitudes and actions have changed over the years, students can interview an elder in the community about the differences between then and now regarding consumer goods.

Materials: notebook or video recorder

Procedure:
This can be a homework assignment or arrangements can be made to have someone come to class to speak with the students. Before the interview, go over the list of questions here and brainstorm some more. Here are some possible questions to ask:

1. What are some of the differences between the kinds of products you use in your home now compared to when you were a child?
2. What are some the ways you used products differently as a child?
3. When you were a child, how were toys different?
4. What were toys and other products made from?
5. Were there ways you shared products more than you do now?
6. What are some products you have now that you did not have as a child?
7. Do you think new products have made life easier?

Once the interviews are completed, students can share their findings and discuss what they learned, what surprised them, and more.

Don't Buy This

The power of advertising has led to an increase in consumerism. As more products are purchased, more products are produced with environmental impact at each step along the way. Buying less stuff not only saves money but also helps lessen our impact on the Earth. Advertisers have developed very successful techniques for getting us to buy the products they are trying to sell and convince us that we need them. Young people are particular targets of advertising and should be aware of how it works.

Materials: advertisements

Procedure:
Have students bring in examples of advertising. This sample can be from all types of media. If it is a television advertisement, they can simply describe the ad or even find it on YouTube. Have them classify the advertisements into groups based on the techniques they use. Some of the major advertising techniques are:

• Nostalgia: Buy this product it and will remind you of the old days when life was simple and good.

• Bandwagon: Buy this product because everyone else is buying it and you want to be like everyone else.

• Fantasy: Buy this product and your dreams will come true.

• Humor: Buy this product because our advertisement is funny.

• Testimonial: Buy this product because a famous person says it is a good idea.

• Statistics: Buy this product because 9 of 10 people say it works.

Take all the advertisements and classify them by the above techniques.

Discuss: What ads do you think work the best? What works the best to get children to buy the products? How can we be aware of advertising tactics? How can you be a smarter consumer? What is the goal of an advertisement?

The 4R Scavenger Hunt

Send students home and/or around the school to find as many ways as possible to:

• Reduce what we use

• Recycle what we use

• Reuse what we use

• Repair what we use

Debate Alternative Energy

There is no one perfect solution to producing the energy we use. Each alternative has pros and cons. What works in one place may not work as well in another. It is important for students to understand that solutions are not always black or white, one or the other.

Materials: resources to research the pros and cons of various forms of alternative energy

Procedure:
Explain the following scenario to the students: Your community is making an effort to become more energy-independent. The town board and the mayor are interested in lowering the costs and the amount of pollution that is generated by the current coal-burning electrical plant. The mayor has invited representatives from companies to speak with the board. The board will decide what to use based on the presentations. You can be the mayor or have some of the students play the town board. Depending on your students and the time available, the assignment can include more detailed reports and presentations. The presentations should include the reasons to support this type of alternative energy and the reason not to support the other kinds. After the students have each made presentations, the board will render a decision.

Alternativeenergysource.org provides information on the pros and cons of various forms of energy at http://www.alternativeenergysource.org/pros_cons.htm. It is a Web site listing the following forms of alternative energy sources and pros and cons for each one.

The California Energy Commission has a lot of ideas for activities. Go to http://www.energy quest.ca.gov/story/chapter17.html for the pros and cons of various sources of alternative energy.

Conserving Peanuts

This is a quick little activity that helps students understand the concept of a non-renewable resource.

Materials: peanuts, candy, or some other item that is small and desirable

Procedure:

Put all the peanuts in a bag so that the students do not know what is inside. Start at one end of the room and let them reach in and take out a handful of peanuts one at a time. When all the peanuts are gone, ask the following discussion questions:

Did everyone get an equal amount?

How does it feel to get more than everyone else?

How does it feel to have less than everyone else?

What will happen to the next class?

What can you do to make the peanuts last longer and still get enough?

Try out the students' plan and see how they were able to carry it out.

Reference

Kriesberg, Daniel A. *A Sense of Place: Teaching Children about the Environment with Picture Books*. Illustrated by Dorothy Frederick. Englewood, CO: Teacher Ideas Press, 1999. 1-56308-565-8.

CHAPTER 5

Pollution

Books

Atwell, Debby. *River*. New York: Houghton Mifflin, 1999. 395-93546-6.

In a folk-art illustration style, Debby Atwell tells the story of one river's changes through the years. Slowly, as more people come to live close to the river, there is more pollution. The animals and plants can no longer survive. Finally, the people realize they have a choice to save the river or let it die. They choose to share and that choice saves the river. The illustrations give the book more depth and detail for discussion.

Bang, Molly. *Chattanooga Sludge: Cleaning Toxic Sludge from Chattanooga Creek*. New York: Harcourt Children's Books, 1996. 015216345X.

Over the years, Chattanooga Creek in Tennessee had become very polluted from factories and other human activities. Instead of giving in, the city council invited a scientist, John Todd, to try out some of his ideas for cleaning polluted water. He created "living machines" that used bacteria, plants, and other organisms to clean polluted water. Not only is this a good book for showing students how water pollution can destroy a river, it also is a good example of how using the scientific method can help people find solutions. Molly Bang's illustrations use a collage technique that brings out many details and brightens the book. Small illustrations along the border of each page provide some background information.

Berger, Carin. *OK Go*. New York: Greenwillow Books, 2009. 978-0-06-157666-9.

This book uses just a handful of different words and fun-filled illustrations. Carin Berger makes a powerful and entertaining statement on the problems of too many cars. The book ends with solutions in the form of suggestions such as "Take a hike, Mike," "Save the planet, Janet," and "Use it again, Jen." After reading the book, students can come up with their own rhymes.

Burns, Loree Griffin. *Tracking Trash: Flotsam, Jetsam, and the Science of Ocean Movement.* Boston: Houghton Mifflin Books, 2007. 0618581316.

Every piece of plastic that is not recycled still exists; it may be in smaller pieces but it is still here. Much of it eventually ends up in the ocean where currents can carry it all over. This book describes the work by scientists who are studying this increasingly serious problem and how it is affecting marine life. There is a good example of how citizen scientists helped researchers better understand how currents are carrying trash. Maps and photographs enliven the text.

Cecil, Laura. *Noah and the Space Ark*. Illustrated by Emma Chichester Clark. Minneapolis, MN: Carolrhoda Books, 1998. 1575052555.

In this story, the world has become so polluted that Noah sees only one option. He builds a space-age ark to take his family and as many animals and plants as possible to an unpolluted place. Readers will enjoy looking at the design of the space ark. When they arrive at the new world, Noah says, "We will take care of it." This book prompts several important questions regarding pollution and other environmental issues. Would we learn from our mistakes if we had a second chance? Can we depend on a technological solution that can take us away from problems? Is it fair that some people can move away from polluted places and others cannot? This may be a picture book but these are issues that are part of dealing with the environmental crisis.

Crelin, Bob. *There Once Was a Sky Full of Stars*. Illustrated by Amie Ziner. Cambridge, MA: Sky Publishing Corp, 2003. 1-931559-04-X.

This book introduces readers to the problems of light pollution in the form of a rhyming poem. The darkness of night is fading due to the increased number of lights that stay on all night. Light pollution may not be as harmful as other forms of pollution but it does have an effect on animals and plants by changing their cycles. As it becomes harder and harder to see the stars, people are losing the wonder and beauty of the night sky.

George, Jean Craighead. *The Case of the Missing Cutthroats*. New York: Harper Collins, 1975. 0-06-025463-3.

This is just one book in a series of ecological mysteries by one of the greatest children's nature writers. With her father, a young girl named Spinner comes to the mountains as a dancer, not a fisherman. She catches the biggest fish, but no one can figure how such a big one could make it downstream and why there are no others. Spinner goes off into the backcountry of the Grand Tetons with her cousin to find out why the big trout she caught survived and all the others are gone. They have a wild adventure and finally figure out why the fish cannot reach the end of the stream. Other books in the series include *The Fire Bug Connection*, 1995; *Who Really Killed Cock Robin*, 1992; and *The Missing Gator of Gumbo Limbo*, 1993.

Greeley, August. *Burning Up*. New York: Power Kids Press, 2003. 0-8239-6482-5.

A simple explanation of the problems associated with the ozone layer that includes the cause, effects, and solution to the problem. The book is illustrated with photographs and diagrams that help to explain what is happening to the ozone layer. The book introduces the Montréal Protocols, which is the international agreement to end the use of chlorofluorocarbon, the chemical that was damaging the ozone layer. Since the hole in the ozone layer is beginning to get smaller, this book can be used to help explain how international cooperation can lead to solving environmental problems.

Hiaasen, Carl. *Flush*. New York: Knopf Books for Young Readers, 2007. 0375841857.

The novel begins with an explosion as Noah's father blows up a gambling boat, the *Coal Queen*, to stop it from dumping waste into the ocean. But instead he ends up in jail. Noah and his sister figure out another way to stop the *Coal Queen* from polluting the waters by using food coloring that traces the waste back to the boat. This is a fun novel with a lot of potential for discussion.

Lloyd, Saci. *The Carbon Diaries*. New York: Holiday House, 2009. 0823421902.

This young adult novel is set in Great Britain in the year 2015. The problems of climate change have become so severe that carbon rationing has begun. Everyone is given an ID card that tracks how much carbon they use each day. Laura must contend with the typical family and teenage issues at a time of great change in her world. Saci Lloyd handles the combination of science fiction with teenage life in the form of a diary. The book paints a picture of what life could be like in a not-so-distant future.

Morichon, David. *Pollution? No Problem!* Brookfield, CT: Millbrook Press, 1994. 0-7613-1260-9.

The animal characters in this book learn an important lesson: there is no way to get rid of the waste we create. Albert has made a machine that produces all sorts of wonderful things. It also makes purple goo, which Albert thinks it will be no problem to throw away. Instead, anywhere he puts the goo, it harms what is around it. Albert realizes the best way to get rid of the purple goo is to stop using the machine.

Pringle, Laurence. *Global Warming: The Threat of Earth's Changing Climate*. New York: Sea Star Books, 2001.

Laurence Pringle writes in a straightforward style that explains the cause and effects of climate change as well as some solutions. The color photographs along with the maps and diagrams help explain this complex issue.

Rockwell, Anne. *What's So Bad about Gasoline? Fossil Fuels and What They Do*. Illustrated by Paul Meisel. New York: HarperCollins, 2009. 978-0-06-157528-0.

This is a very useful book for explaining the impact of gasoline and other fossil fuels on the planet. The book is a time line that explains how fossil fuels were formed millions of years ago, how they have been used since ancient times, and how they are used today. It is at this stage of the time line that fossil fuels are having such a negative impact on the environment. The book ends with some information on possible solutions to the negative effects of fossil fuels.

Thompson, Colin. *The Tower to the Sun*. New York: Alfred A. Knopf, 1997. 0-679-88334-7.

The Earth has become so polluted that sunshine cannot get through the clouds. The world's richest man wants his grandson to feel and see the sun. To get past the clouds of pollution, they build a tower through the clouds to where the sun still shines. The tower is made from a collection of famous buildings from all over the world, all intricately drawn by the author. This book can inspire discussion about what happened and how the construction of the tower could help or hurt the situation.

Thornhill, Jan. *This Is My Planet: The Kids' Guide to Global Warming*. Toronto: Maple Tree Press, 2007. 978-1-897349-06-9.

This is an excellent book for teaching students about climate change and a good source of understandable information for any adult trying to better understand the problem. The book begins by explaining the key interrelationships and cycles one needs to know to understand climate change. Photographs and diagrams help to do this in an effective manner. The next part of the book reviews the effects climate change is having around the planet and the effects that are likely to occur in the future. This can be a scary topic, but the straightforward facts help to keep it in perspective. The book ends with a focus on what can be done to help, including both lifestyle changes and new technology.

Wells, Robert. *Polar Bear, Why Is Your World Melting?* Morton Grove, IL: Albert Whitman & Company, 2008. 978-0-8075-6598-8.

Robert Wells describes our planet as a "Goldilocks World," not too hot and not too cold, but just right. Beginning with the polar bears and their plight, this book provides a simple explanation of climate change, the causes, the effects, and some solutions. One of the important concepts the book introduces is how feedback interrelationships increase the effects of climate change. Ice reflects heat back into space, which keeps the earth cooler. As more ice melts, less heat is reflected and more is absorbed, which increases the temperature, which makes more ice melt and so on. The additional background information is presented with cartoon-like illustrations that convey the information with less of the fear factor.

Activities

To understand pollution, it is helpful to understand some basic chemistry. Most people tend to think of chemicals as something negative, poisonous, and dangerous, but in fact, everything is a chemical. Living and non-living things are all made from different chemical combinations of atoms, just as words are made up from different combinations of letters. When combined with other atoms, matter can be rearranged to make new kinds of matter, just as the letters in two words can be rearranged to make new words. When atoms recombine to make new matter, it is called a chemical change.

Chemical changes happen all the time in the natural world. Photosynthesis is how plants change water, carbon dioxide, and sunlight into oxygen and sugars. Digestion is a chemical change in which the food that is eaten becomes the body of the animal. By creating and making chemical changes in raw materials, we make the products we use. The reason there is pollution is that we have created combinations of atoms that are harmful to living things. In some cases, we have done this deliberately, such as with pesticides, and in other instances, the toxic chemicals are by-products of the things we are making. We have created so many of these substances and in such large amounts that the problem has become widespread. In addition, since these chemicals are made by humans, they cannot be decomposed through natural processes. This means that they last a very long time. In other cases, our actions have increased amounts of naturally occurring chemicals such as carbon dioxide to such a degree that they are also causing problems.

Life on Earth depends on the interrelationships between the lithosphere, the hydrosphere, the atmosphere, the land, water, and air. Each one influences the other and is influenced by the other. The cycles of elements and the lives of all living things interact through each sphere. Because of this, we cannot simply think of air pollution affecting only the air, water pollution affecting only the water, or land pollution affecting only the land—everyplace is impacted.

Pollution Awareness

Materials: none

Procedure:
As students go through their daily routine, they pay attention and look for examples of pollution.

Understanding Pollution: Wonderful Water

Materials: glasses, lemonade mix, ice cubes, paper towels

Procedure:

To grasp the problem of water pollution, it helps to understand the importance and uniqueness of water. There is no substitute for water, and there is a limited amount. Without water, life would not exist as we know it today. Making a glass of lemonade demonstrates some of water's unique properties.

1. Give each child a glass of water and an ice cube.

2. Ask them to put the ice cube in the glass. A floating ice cube may not seem like much, but it is a unique phenomenon: the solid water floats on the liquid water. There is no other matter in which the solid state of the substance floats on the liquid state of the substance. (For example, a copper penny sinks in a glass of melted copper.) Solid water has less density than liquid water. What makes this important is that if ice were heavier than water, ponds and lakes would freeze from the bottom up, killing most of the life in the water.

3. Pour in the lemonade. What happens? The lemonade dissolves. Another important quality of water is its ability to dissolve other matter, including oxygen. Without dissolved oxygen in water, animals would not be able to survive.

4. Leave some lemonade out to evaporate over the course of a couple of days. The amazing thing is that within the normal range of temperatures on Earth, water can be in the liquid, solid, and gaseous form. Water is the only matter that can do this. Without this property, water could not be recycled. The water cycle allows Earth to maintain life with a limited amount of water.

5. Spill a little lemonade on the table. Use a paper towel to soak it up. Watch the water move through the paper towel. One molecule pulls another upward. Water is very cohesive, which means water molecules stick together. Without this property, water would not be able to rise up from the roots of plants hundreds of feet into the air. If water cannot reach the leaves, photosynthesis cannot take place, and therefore no food is produced. These properties give us a clue as to the value of water.

What Is Air?

Understanding air pollution begins with understanding air. Air is a mixture of gases. Nitrogen makes up 78 percent of the air and oxygen makes up 21 percent. These are followed by argon .93 percent, carbon dioxide .03 percent, and the rest trace gases and water vapor. Each gas has its own unique properties and plays a different role in how air supports life on Earth. The following simple chemistry activities will demonstrate that different gases have different properties and that two kinds of matter can change into a new kind of matter.

If you do not have enough equipment for all the students to work together, these activities can be done as demonstrations. These experiments require students to be very aware of safety procedures. You will need safety goggles for everyone who is directly participating in the experiment.

Making Oxygen

Materials: for each group of students, a test tube, a test tube stopper, matches, wooden splints, beaker with water, a test tube holder, hydrogen peroxide, and yeast

Procedure:

1. Set up a test tube in a test tube holder.
2. Pour in 2 ml of yeast.
3. Pour in 2 ml of hydrogen peroxide.
4. Put the stopper on the test tube without pushing it in.
5. The mixture will quickly bubble, producing oxygen.
6. Light the splint and blow out the flame to get a glowing ember on the end.
7. Put the match in the beaker with water.
8. Stick the glowing splint in the test tube.

The splint should burst back into flames; students can blow out the flame and put the ember in the test tube again. Repeat until all the oxygen in the test tube has been used up.
What is happening?

Hydrogen peroxide is a molecule made from two oxygen atoms and two hydrogen atoms. The yeast acts as a catalyst to split apart the hydrogen and oxygen molecules, changing the hydrogen peroxide from H_2O_2 into H_2 and O_2. If the amount of oxygen in the air were to increase, it would make it much harder to put out fires. So far Earth has been able to keep the balance.

Making Carbon Dioxide

Materials: for each group of students, a test tube, a test tube stopper, matches, wooden splints, beaker with water, a test tube holder, baking soda, and vinegar

Procedure:

1. Set up a test tube into a test tube holder.
2. Pour in 3 ml of baking soda.
3. Pour in 3 ml of vinegar.
4. Put a stopper on top of the test tube.
5. The mixture will react quickly, producing carbon dioxide.
6. Light the splint and place the match in the beaker of water.
7. Put the flaming splint in the test tube but not into the bubbles.
8. The flame should go out.
9. Students can relight the splint and put it into the test tube again. When the flame goes out again, what does this tell you about the density of carbon dioxide compared to air? (Carbon dioxide is denser then air and will stay in the test tube even with stopper off.)
   What happens? Baking soda ($NaHCO_3$) + vinegar (CH_3COOH) becomes carbon dioxide (CO_2) + water (H_2O) + sodium acetate (CH_3COONa).

Each gas has its own properties, and the air is a balance of all these different gases. When there is too much or too little of one part, it will throw off the balance and cause negative effects for life on Earth.

Causes of Air Pollution

Cars, trucks, buses, and other vehicles are major causes of pollution. Even when vehicles are not moving, they are still causing pollution. Idling itself is a major cause of air pollution. Idling a car engine for 10 minutes produces one pound of carbon dioxide.

Materials: none

Procedure:
Students look for examples of unnecessary idling at school, at home, and in their neighborhoods. Discuss where they have observed the most unnecessary idling. If possible, station students outside the school at the beginning and end of the day to find out how long people idle while dropping off or picking up their children.

Extensions:
How many cars are in the school parking lot for every adult in the school?
How many cars drive by the school in one hour? What would your estimate be for one week? What is the average number of people in each car? How can we encourage more people to carpool?

How Far Can Your Car Go?

The better the gas mileage, the less pollution a car produces. Gas mileage is expressed in miles per gallon (mpg), which measures the number of miles a car can drive on one gallon of gas.

Materials: family automobile

Procedure: To figure out the mpg for a car, follow these steps:

What Is Your Gas Mileage?

1. Fill up the gas tank.
2. What is the mileage?
3. Drive until the tank is less than half full. Fill up the tank again.
4. How many gallons did it take to fill up tank?
5. What is the mileage?
6. Subtract to find the number of miles you drove since the last fill-up.
7. Divide your answer (the number of miles driven) by the number of gallons it took to fill up your tank. This is your car's mpg.

The average car produces 20 pounds of carbon dioxide for each gallon of gas burned.

United States Environmental Protection Agency. "Emission Facts: Average Carbon Dioxide Emissions Resulting From Gas and Diesel Fuel," http://www.epa.gov/oms/climate/420f05001.htm#calculating.

Extensions:
How can you increase your mpg?
Does the car get better gas mileage with different brands of gas?
How does your actual mpg compare to what the car dealer says the mpg will be?

Electrical Generation

It takes just a quick look around the classroom or house to get an idea of how much electricity we use on a daily basis.

Most of our electricity is made by spinning a huge magnet inside a large coil of wire. A turbine is used to spin the magnet. To spin the turbine, something must push it. Most of the electricity in the United States is generated by using steam to spin the turbine. To have steam, water must be heated hot enough to change into a gas. To heat the water, something must burn. By far the most commonly used fuel is coal. These power plants are a major source of air pollution. More than 40 percent of the total U.S. carbon dioxide emissions comes from burning coal. Burning coal also emits air pollutants such as lead, arsenic, and mercury. The particulate matter that is produced causes a host of health problems in humans and damages crops and other plant life.

Sierra Club. "The Dirty Truth about Coal: Why Yesterday's Technology Should Not Be Part of Tomorrow's Energy Future." May 2008. http://www.sierraclub.org/coal/downloads/0508-coal-report-fact-sheet.pdf.

Mining coal also has a number of environmental impacts on land and water as well as air. Large amounts of water are used in the process of taking the coal out of the ground. Water is polluted by the mine tailings, and there is a huge amount of solid waste produced.

The United States Environmental Protection Agency. "Clean Energy Coal." December 28, 2007. http://www.epa.gov/RDEE/energy-and-you/affect/coal.html.

Materials: bar magnet, copper wire, toilet paper roll, compasses

Procedure:
An electrical current will cause a compass needle to move, which makes a compass a simple tool for observing electrical currents. Wrap the wire around the toilet paper roll about 20 to 30 times. Wrap the ends of the wire around a compass. Move the magnet back and forth inside the toilet paper tube to create a small amount of electricity.

Extensions:
Challenge students to make an electrical generator powerful enough to light a small lightbulb. What other ways can they invent to spin the turbine? How can we design the turbine so that it needs less energy to spin the magnet? What are other ways to generate electricity?

Electricity in the House

Procedure: Have the students count how many items in their house use electricity. Ask them to talk to their parents about how many items in their house used electricity when they were children. Discuss what it would be like to go one day without electricity. What would you miss the most? What could you easily do without?

Watershed History Lesson

Water does not just become instantly polluted. There is a story that explains how a lake, stream, river, or other body of water becomes polluted. To demonstrate this, you can create a mini-watershed. These lessons are most effective when you use a body of water in the community and tell the story with details from local history.

Materials: bowl of water, pieces of wood, sawdust, small pieces of metal, cooking oil, powders, and other materials to represent toxic chemicals such as fertilizers, oil, and pesticides; toilet paper to represent human waste; and some small objects to represent fish and other food resources in the water

Procedure:
Tell the class you are taking them on trip back in time to show them what happened to Lake _____ (pick a body of water near your community).

Step one: Say, "This bowl of water represents the lake before any human contact." Put in some plastic cubes or some other item to represent fish.
Step two: Say, "Native people lived in the area. What kinds of pollution did they add to the lake?" Anything they added was biodegradable and did not have much of an impact on the water. They also fished and gathered other food from the lake, but since their population was relatively low, there were plenty of fish left. Add some pieces of wood to symbolize how Native Americans affected the lake. To demonstrate how the lake was used, take one fish out.
Step three: Say, "About 500 years ago, the Europeans came. What did they add?" They added more human waste, there was an increase in hunting and fishing, and some wetlands were filled in. Still, overall the impact was limited. To demonstrate, add more wood and a little metal and take out more fish.
Step four: Say, "Time goes on, and it is now around 1870, and the Industrial Revolution is in full swing. What is being put into the water?" Now there is pollution from the factories that are built along the lake. There is an increase in human population that leads to increase human waste. Over-fishing is beginning to take place. Along the lake, trees are being cut down in increased numbers and erosion is washing soil into the water. The water quality is beginning to decline. To demonstrate, add paper, wood, and soil and take out five fish.
Step five: Say, "After World War II, conditions change even more. There are more factories and industries. Now what is happening to the water?" The factories are located near water for production and shipping. The industries are using materials that are not biodegradable, and many are toxic to fish and other living things. The human population has increased greatly, and most water treatment plants are not able to clean the wastewater properly. More and more fish are being taken from the waters, and in some cases, it is no longer safe to eat the fish from the lake or drink the water.
To demonstrate, add powders, oil, toilet paper, and other substances to the water and take out all the remaining fish.
Step six: Say, "It is today, now what?"

Oil Spills

Materials: water, cooking oil, feather

Procedure:
Put the feather in the water and record the observations. Put a little oil in the water and on the feather. Place the feather in the water and observe happens. Try to get the oil off the feather. What happens? How would this affect a bird's ability to survive?

Garbage Graveyard

Some of our garbage decomposes and some lasts a very long time. The problem is that most of the garbage we throw away is the kind that lasts a long time. This garbage takes up open land, and dangerous chemicals can leach into the ground.

Materials: various items of garbage

Procedure:
The students make signs for different types of garbage that explain how long it will take for the garbage to decompose. This information can be displayed as a bulletin board. However, a more effective lesson can be taught by making an actual garbage graveyard outdoors. It is interesting to dig up the items on occasion to observe how much they have changed over time. Remember, breaking up into smaller pieces is not the same as decomposing. Here are some examples that students can use along with the time it takes for each item to decompose.

• Paper: two to four weeks

• Banana peel: three to five weeks

• Plastic bottle or plastic bag: 500-plus years

• Wool hat: one year

• Apple core: one week

• Cigarette butt: one to five years

• Disposable diaper: 10 to 20 years

• Hard plastic container: 20 to 30 years

• Aluminum can: 80 to 200 years

• Glass bottles: forever

Weather.com. Forecast Earth. "In a Landfill, How Long Does Trash Really Last?" by Brie Cadman. http://climate.weather.com/articles/dclandfill2009.html.

Litter Lookout

Materials: garbage bags, garden gloves, two cones

Procedure:
Students walk their neighborhood and school grounds to pick up litter. As they fill their bags, they should keep track how many pieces of each type of litter they find. After throwing it away, discuss the types of litter they found and ways to reduce the amount of garbage based on what their findings. Another way to do this activity is to ask the custodian at the school to save a bag or two of garbage. Students can dissect the bag and discuss ways of reducing the amount of garbage.

Acid Rain

Acid precipitation is caused from the burning of fossil fuels such as coal and oil. Sulfur from the burning fuel combines with oxygen to make sulfur dioxide. Exhaust from cars forms into nitrogen oxides. These gases dissolve in water vapor and become sulfuric acid and nitric acid. When these chemical compounds fall back to Earth in the form of rain, snow, sleet, hail, or any precipitation, they can change the chemical makeup of bodies of water and damage forests. The pollutants can come from far away and are carried by wind from one place to another. For more information, go to the United Sates Geographical Survey's Web site on acid rain at http://ga.water.usgs.gov/edu/acid rain.html.

Acid Rain Game

Materials: 24 index cards—label four cards as sulfur dioxide, four cards as nitrous oxide, eight cards as water, and eight cards as fish. If you have extra students, simply make more fish cards.

Procedure:
This game is best played outdoors, but the children can walk through the game if played indoors. Mark out three areas. The first is where the gases from cars and factories come out. Mark this with two cones about six feet apart. Students with pollution cards stand here. Mark out an area as a cloud; this is where students with water cards stand. Mark out the third area as a pond; the fish will go here. Set up boundaries so when the students are being chased, they do not run out of the cloud or out of the pond.

First, the pollutants run out of the factories and cars between the cones and chase the water molecules in the cloud area. Once a water molecule is tagged by a pollutant, it becomes acid precipitation. They now run into the pond with linked arms and tag a fish. When the fish is tagged, it "dies" and leaves the pond to stand next to you. Just a reminder: acid rain does not get on the fish and kill them; it changes the chemical makeup of the water, which then kills the fish. Another option is to have the fish die a dramatic death when all the acid precipitation pairs have run into the pond area. The game ends when all the fish are dead.

Discuss what can be done so that there is less pollution coming out of the factories and cars. Scrubbers are one technique used to filter out much of the pollutants. To simulate a scrubber, have one student stand in front of the cones where the pollutants come out. If the scrubber tags a pollutant before it gets to the cloud, the pollutant has to go back, count to 10, and try again. Play the game with the scrubber for the same amount of time as without and compare how many fish are killed. Why wouldn't an electric company use a scrubber? These techniques have proved effective in helping to decrease the problems of acid rain.

Pollution Indicators

Unfortunately, there is pollution in the air we breathe. By learning where the highest concentration of pollution is, we can take more effective steps to limit its impact. These pollution indicators will help students find out what is in the air.

Materials: petroleum jelly, petri dishes (or something similar)

Procedure:
Spread petroleum jelly over the bottom of the dishes. Make a chart to record the location of the dishes and the observations the students make. Place the dishes in different places inside and outside the school. Leave them out for a night if possible. Check the dishes and record the results. Put the dishes out again and record a second round of observations.

Discuss:

What are the most polluted spots at school?

Why do you think some places are more polluted than other spots?

What can be done?

Water Detectives

Water pollution comes from either non-point or point sources. Non-point pollution means that the pollutants are not flowing into the water from one specific spot. The pollutants are running off the land over a wide area. Some examples of non-point pollution are fertilizer runoff from agricultural lands or oil dripping out of cars and trucks and being washed into the water. Point sources are when the pollution is coming from one specific place. This type of water pollution is easier to control in most cases since the source of the pollution is clear.

In this activity, students set up a mock situation in which they are detectives trying to figure why and how the lake in their town is being polluted. The scenario is that the lake is suffering from higher-than-normal amounts of nitrogen. There are several possible reasons for this based on the actions of some of the people living near the lake. The students will have to figure who and what is causing the high levels of nitrogen.

<u>Step one:</u>

Materials: none

Procedure:
Explain to students that many people are reporting problems about conditions in and around the lake. For example:

Mr. Jones reports that when he goes fishing, he rarely catches fish anymore.

Mrs. Parker says that she has noticed more algae growing on the rocks.

Mr. Lee reports that he sees fewer birds.

Mrs. Reynolds reports that it is hard to go snorkeling because the water is so cloudy.

You can report these observations to the students yourself or take some of them aside and assign them roles to play to report the information. After hearing the information, the students can take the necessary steps to figure out what is going on and how they can help.

<u>Step two:</u>

Materials: water samples, water test kits

Procedure:
Is there something wrong with the water in the lake? Just because people make these observations does not mean there is a problem. Scientists need more facts before acting. Bring in a beaker of water and tell the students it is from the lake and they are going to run some tests on it to see if they can figure out if anything is out of balance.

Use a simple water test kit to analyze the water. The Green Low Cost Water Monitoring Kit from LaMotte is good. There are other water testing kits that can be used for a more in-depth study at http://www.lamotte.com/component/option,com_pages/lang,en/mid,/page,69/task,item.

To make the role-play more realistic, add a touch of fertilizer or a little ammonia to the water to get a high reading for nitrates.

After the students have tested the water sample and recorded the results, they have their first fact. The lake has high nitrogen levels. Keep a list of all the factors on a large sheet of chart paper.

<u>Step three:</u>

How did the increased nitrogen get into the lake? To make the mystery more fun, use some teachers as suspects. If the students are going to be the heroes of the story, there needs to be a villain. Create four possible suspects from people who live around the lake. The suspects could be fictionalized teachers or you can use real ones, just be sure you have their permission. Put photographs or pictures of the suspects on a bulletin board using the following quotes to set up the situation. If possible, adapt the quotes to your local situation.

"I am expanding my golf course and restaurant. Why would I pollute the lake?"

"I run sailboat races. Why would I pollute the lake?"

"I just built 14 new houses. Why would I pollute the lake?"

"My marina does great business. Why would I pollute the lake?"

Before anyone can be convicted, more evidence is needed. The students will go through a series of crime scene analysis activities to find out who is polluting the lake.

<u>Step four:</u>

A white powder is found on the shoreline of the lake. A sample has been brought back to the lab for analysis. To figure out what the powder is, the students will study its properties and compare them to properties of other white powders.

Materials: salt, sugar, baking soda, baking powder, flour, and other white powders; small cups or dishes to hold powders, spoons, hand lens, data sheet, vinegar, flasks, iodine, water

Procedure:

Hand out copies of the powder chart to each group. Show them the various powders they will be comparing to the mystery powder. Students should take a small sample of each powder and observe the texture, hand lens, reaction to vinegar and iodine, solubility, and any other characteristics. To record its reaction to vinegar, the students put a few drops of vinegar on the powder and observe. They do the same thing with a couple of drops of iodine. To measure solubility, students dissolve the powders in water and observe the results.

Powder Tests

	Hand Lens	Texture	Reaction to Vinegar	Solubility	Reaction to iodine	Other
Flour						
Baking Soda						
Sugar						
Salt						
Baking Powder						
Mystery Powder						

At the end, they run the same tests on the mystery powder. Use the chart to compare the properties of the powders. The students decide which one matches best with the mystery powder. On a piece of chart paper, record this fact along with any other new data.

Step five:

Materials: paper towels, beakers, at least four magic markers (all the same color)

Procedure:
Tell the students you found a map showing some plans for development around the lake. Prior to class, draw the map using one of the markers.

Show them the map and explain that we can find out what markers made the map by using paper chromatography. Paper chromatography is technique scientists use to separate the parts of a mixture. In this case, the ink from the marker is a mixture of colors, and each brand of marker has a unique mix of inks. A solvent such as water is used to separate the different colors of the ink. Each brand of marker dissolves in a unique pattern.

Have each group of students cut four strips of paper towels about four inches long and three-quarters of an inch wide. They draw a line with each marker on a different strip. Be sure they label which line is which marker. Meanwhile, cut strips off the map and give one to each group. The students fill a glass half way with water and place the strips in the water with the ink far enough from the end so that the water has to move through the paper towel and dissolve the ink. Once the ink is dissolved into its pattern, they can compare the stripes they made with the sample from the map to determine which marker was used to draw the map. Add this fact to the list of clues.

Step six:

Announce you found a note that reads, "I hope no one found the map." To determine who wrote the note, the students can analyze the handwriting. Prior to the class, have each teacher (suspect) write "I hope no one found the map" on the same sheet of paper. Have the teacher (suspect) who committed the crime write the sentence on the bottom, with slightly different handwriting. Make copies of the sheet and hand them out along with the data sheet.

Properties to analyze for handwriting analysis: slant, spacing between letters, spacing between words, size, and style.

Once the students have figured out who wrote the note, add this fact to the list of clues.

Step seven:

Since there are high levels of nitrogen, the students should also learn more about the effects of nitrogen. This brief explanation can be supplemented with additional research by the students.

Surplus nitrogen causes a problem called hypoxia. High nitrogen levels are caused by increased amounts of human waste and from fertilizer that has run off from farms, lawns, golf courses, etc. The increase in nitrogen acts as a fertilizer, increasing plant growth in the water. When the plants die, there is a surge in bacteria population and decomposers that in turn use up more oxygen. With less oxygen in the water the fish die off or swim away.

Add these facts to the list of clues. Using the clues, the students should now develop a list of questions for the suspects that will help them gain more information. Just because someone drew a map doesn't mean they are polluting the lake.

Step eight:

Depending on the teachers' ability to role-play, you can either have the teachers visit your classroom and the students ask them questions directly or you can answer the questions yourself. Have the answers lead them to conclusion that Mrs. _____ has been secretly trying to expand her golf course. She was saving money for the project, so when the septic tank broke, she did not fix it, which led to more human waste going in the water. She increased the amount of fertilizer to make her course greener for better sales and this increased the water's nitrogen levels. The white powder was baking powder she was using in her restaurant and it was stuck to her shoes. She left some behind when she was by the water mapping out the project.

What suggestions do the students have to help Mrs. _____ expand the golf course without hurting the lake?

Water Testing

Materials: water test kits, samples of water from local ponds, streams, lakes

Procedure:
Have the students use the test kits and record the results on a data sheet. After gathering the information, they can use it to measure the health of local water bodies. World Water Monitoring Day is an international organization that promotes awareness and action to protect water resources by involving citizens in water monitoring activities. This a great way to get your students involved as well. http://www.worldwatermonitoringday.org/index.html.

Indicator Species

One way scientists observe the effects of pollution is by studying indicator species. Indicator species are animals and plants that are sensitive to changes in their habitat caused by pollution. Scientists collect animals from a study site and identify the species. Some organisms can tolerate living in polluted areas while others require places with very little pollution. Depending on the animals and plants living in the ecosystem, scientists can determine the health of that ecosystem. Aquatic habitats are particularly good places for studying indicator species.

Materials: nets, trays, identifying sheets, spoons

Procedure:

Step one: Collecting animal specimens
Collect aquatic animals at a pond, lake, or stream. Begin by using pond nets to scoop up water and leaves. Place everything in trays and have the students carefully look through the leaves and muck with a spoon. When they see any aquatic invertebrates, they carefully pick them up and place them in a tray with clear water. When the tray has been searched carefully, put the leaves back in the water and give them a new batch to look through. If you can't bring the students to a pond, lake, or stream, you can bring a bucketful of leaves and muck to the classroom. If you do not have access to a pond, another option is to use photographs of aquatic invertebrates to create a community with a varying population of animals. For more information, the Environmental Protection Agency has a Web site on indicator species at http://www.epa.gov/bioindicators/html/indicator.html. There you can find background information and photographs of the animals.

This Web site from the Izaak Walton League is also a good source of information and photographs. www.iwla.org

Step two: Measuring the health of the water
Use the following key to identify the animals the students have captured. *The Golden Guide to Pond Life* is also a helpful resource for identification and information. Once the animals are identified, count how many there are of each species. Multiply the number of individuals by their biotic index value. Then add up all the biotic values and divide by the number of individuals.

Carefully return all the creatures to the water when the activity is completed. The students can then write report describing their findings.

Bioindicators

	Biotic Index Value
Group One: These organisms are pollution-intolerant.	
Stonefly nymph	10
Caddisfly larva	10
Dobsonfly nymph	10
Mayfly nymph	10
Water scorpion	10
Group Two: These organisms live in a wide range of water qualities.	
Dragonfly nymph	6
Sowbug	6
Crayfish	6
Blackfly larva	6
Scud	6
Diving beetle	8
Fingernail clam	6
Group Three: These organisms are generally tolerant of pollution:	
Midge larva	4
Aquatic worm	4
Leech	4
Snail	4
Isopod	4

Scale of Water Quality
Excellent: > 8
Good: 6–7
Fair: 4–5
Poor: < 4

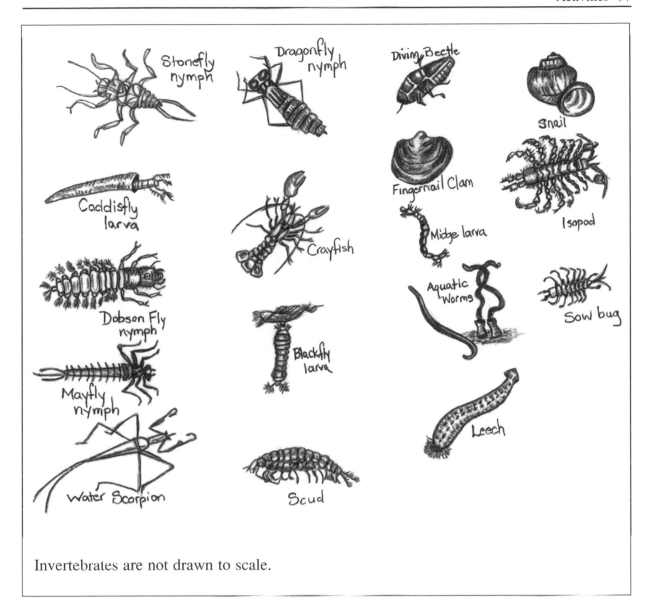

Invertebrates are not drawn to scale.

Water Treatment

A trip to the nearest water treatment plant would the best way to learn how water is cleaned. If the students cannot go, they can take this virtual tour by cleaning their own sewage. These are the main steps taken in a wastewater treatment plant to clean water to be released back into a river, lake, or ocean.

Model Sewage Treatment

This model gives children a peek inside some the steps to clean water.

Materials: "sewage," two soda bottles (one with the top cut off), alum, screen or strainer

Procedure:
Make the sewage water by mixing 2 and 1/2 cups of dirt with 1 gallon of water. You can add some other "sewage" as well such as food waste, small bits of plastic, other liquids, and more.

1. Aeration: The sewage is shaken and exposed to air. This causes some of dissolved gases that taste and smell bad to be released from the water. Air is also pumped through the sewage to add oxygen, which helps the bacteria decompose the organic materials. This also helps the organic materials separate from the sand and other dense particles.
   Shake the bottle for about 30 seconds and then pour the water back and forth between another bottle at least 10 times. Pour the aerated water into the bottle with the top cut off.

2. Screening: The water is filtered to remove large items such as wood, rocks, and large pieces of garbage. Pull an old comb across the water to take off large items.

3. Coagulation: In the next step, the sludge (organic material) settles out of the sewage and is pumped from the tanks. Dirt and other suspended particles become clumped together with alum to make it easier to separate from the water. To demonstrate, add two tablespoons of alum to the water and stir for five minutes. The clumps will be easier to screen out.

4. Sedimentation: While the sludge is settling to the bottom, lighter materials float to the top. Rakes skim off the scum. It is then thickened and pumped into digesters along with the sludge.

5. Let the water stand for 20 minutes to separate the materials by density.

6. Filtration: Another round of filtration is used to clear off more sediment. Put sand, coarse sand, pebbles, and coffee filters into a funnel and pour the water through several times.

7. Chlorination: Chlorine is added to the water to kill bacteria.

8. Discharge: Now the water is ready to be discharged. It goes back into the ocean or local river or lake.

Compare the filtered water to the unfiltered water.

Climate Change

Teaching the effects of climate change can be scary and disheartening. Be mindful of the age of your students and begin by focusing simply on understanding climate change before teaching about the causes. Be sure to include solutions as part of the lessons.

Making Greenhouses

Materials: trays, plastic wrap, thermometers
Without some greenhouse effect, life could not exist on our planet. The atmosphere traps heat from the sun and keeps Earth at temperatures that allow life. Human activity has added so much greenhouse gas

that the chemical makeup of the atmosphere has changed enough so that more heat is being trapped and there has been a slight rise in Earth's temperature.

To demonstrate this, put thermometers in a box or tray. Record the starting temperature. Wrap one box with a couple of sheets of clear plastic wrap. Put the boxes in the sun or under a lamp. After a half an hour, open the plastic and record the temperature.

Climate Versus Weather

One key to understanding climate change is to understand the difference between weather and climate. Weather is the condition of the atmosphere regarding rain, wind, and temperature; climate is the prevailing weather, conditions of the place, and the average weather over time. Scientists have come to the conclusion that the overall temperature of the Earth has risen and continues to do so. That doesn't mean there will not be a cold winter or record cold temperatures on occasion. That is an example of weather. Understanding these words is a good example of why everyone should know basic science so they can grasp what is going on and make good decisions.

Materials: newspapers, almanacs

Procedure:
Students take an imaginary trip around the world, stopping at least 10 places in one day. At each stop, they will record the weather of the day and find out the climate. Share the results and discuss the differences between climate and weather. Students can make a weather and climate report of their travels.

Biography of a Gas

Materials: research materials

Procedure:
Students select one greenhouse gas, such as carbon dioxide, water vapor, methane, or nitrous oxide, and write a biography based on the information they gather. They should try to find out what the gas made from, its impact, and what can we do to prevent it from causing more problems. Once they have the information, they create a poster to display their work.

What Are the Best Web Sites for Teaching Climate Change?

There are a number of Web sites with games and activities to help children understand the issues of climate change. Your students can evaluate the effectiveness of these sites.

Materials: computers with an Internet connection

Procedure:
Give students time to explore and try these Web sites. They should develop a list of criteria on which to base their evaluations. Here is a list to begin with, but your students will find others:

• Who developed the Web site?

• How is the Web site funded?

• Is the information accurate?

• Are the activities fun?

• Are the activities interesting?

• What did you learn from the Web site?

Green Car Purchase

Materials: research materials

Procedure:
Since automobiles are such an environmental problem, purchasing environmentally responsible cars makes sense. The students can use the following Web sites and others to gather information they need to decide which environmentally friendly car is best. Besides environmental impacts, they should also consider the kind of car they would choose given their lifestyle.

These Web sites from the Environmental Protection Agency can help people find the best car to buy to reduce greenhouse gases: http://www.epa.gov/greenvehicles/Index.do and http://www.fueleconomy.gov/FEG/bymodel/bymakemodelNF.shtml.

Environmental Defense Fund. "Attention Drivers! Turn Off Your Idling Engine." http://www.edf.org/page.cfm?tagID=22292.

CHAPTER 6

Activities for Action

Books

Anderson, Joan. *Earth Keepers*. Photographs by George Ancona. New York: Harcourt Brace & Company, 1993. 0-15-242199-8.

This book chronicles the work of three different organizations and their efforts to help protect the environment. The book begins with the story of the sloop *Clearwater* and the Hudson River. Over the years, the Hudson River had become terribly polluted. The *Clearwater* sails the Hudson, educating adults and children about the river. They were instrumental in focusing attention on and helping to change the way people treated the river. Today, the Hudson River is dramatically cleaner and in many ways has been restored. The other stories in this book feature the work of Malinda Futrell and Nancy Paye and their efforts to create vegetable and flower gardens in empty lots in New York City. There is also the story of Lynn Rogers, a wildlife biologist who has made it his life's work to understand how animals live. These stories of environmental heroes will serve as models for students. As a follow-up, students can find out the status of the work currently being done by these Earth-keepers.

Bongiorno, Lori. *Green, Greener, Greenest: A Practical Guide to Making Eco-Smart Choices a Part of Your Life*. New York: Perigee Book, 2008. 978-0-399-53403-4.

The ideas in this book cover a variety of areas from what we eat, how we shop, what we wear, to what's inside our homes. Each chapter includes helpful background information on the issues. The action ideas are organized by the positive impact they will have. There are the green ideas, which are a simple way to get started, followed by the greener ideas, which take the next step. These are followed by the greenest ideas; they take the most commitment but will also have the greatest impact.

Bruchac, Joseph. *Rachel Carson: Preserving a Sense of Wonder*. Illustrated by Thomas Locker. 2009. 1555916953.

Rachel Carson is wonderful example of an environmental hero. She combined powerful writing, a strong background in science, and a sense of wonder to write a book that many feel started the modern environmental movement. *Silent Spring* brought the problems of DDT and other pesticides to national attention. This biography will show your students how one person and the power of words can make a difference.

Burch, Joann. J. *Chico Mendes, Defender of the Rainforest*. Brookfield, CT: Millbrook Press, 1994. 1-5629413-4.

Chico Mendes' life was cut short when he was killed working to protect the rain forests of Brazil. This biography follows the events of his life as he changed from a young boy just learning to read to an environmental activist trying to protect the rainforest. What makes this such a powerful story is the fact that Mendes was not just working to protect the animals and plants of the rain forest; he was also working to protect the people who called the rain forest their home. This book is part of Gateway Greens, a series of biographies about various environmental activists.

Burleigh, Robert. *Into the Woods: John James Audubon Lives His Dream*. Illustrated by Wendell Minor. New York: Atheneum Books, 2003. 0-689-83040-8.

John James Audubon was a painter who life's ambition was to paint every bird species in North America. His pictures captured the details, actions, and color of birds and other wildlife. His work celebrated the wildlife and wilderness of the United States at a time when most Americans saw the wilderness as a dark, evil place, and wildlife as something to exploit. This book combines entries from his journals with an imaginary letter that Audubon might have written to his father explaining his life choices. Together they capture the dreams and thoughts of a painter who inspired so many others with his work.

Callery, Sean. *Victor Wouk: The Father of the Hybrid Car*. New York: Crabtree Publishing Company, 2009. 978-0-7787-4677-5.

Victor Wouk is a good example of how someone can help the environment by inventing new technology. His work in the 1970s on developing hybrid cars was well ahead of its time. One can only wonder how much cleaner the environment would be if he had been given more support by the Environmental Protection Agency. He helped lead the way to the development of the hybrid cars of today. The information about his childhood helps students to see how their interests can lead to careers that make a difference.

Cheng, Christopher. *One Child*. Illustrated by Steven Woolman. Northampton, MA: Crocodile Books, 2000. 1-56656-330-5.

In the face of a polluted planet, a child asks, "What can I do?" With beautiful, simple text and dramatic illustrations, the child is able to answer the question. As others take small but important actions, color images take over the sober black-and-white illustrations, helping the reader to imagine the possibilities.

Child, Lauren. *What Planet Are You From, Clarice Bean?* Cambridge, MA: Candlewick Press, 2002. 0-7636-1696-6.

A wonderfully, quirky book that is hard to describe in which Clarice is determined to save the tree growing near her home from being cut down. At the same time, she tries to stay out of trouble with her teacher. The illustrations come alive with color and story as Clarice finds a way to save the tree. There are humorous side comments, ecology tips, and a sense of adventure.

Collard, Sneed B. *Butterfly Count.* Illustrated by Paul Kratter. New York: Holiday House, 2002 0-8234-1607-0.

This is a great book to use with any environmental-monitoring project or just as an example of what people can do to protect endangered wildlife in their communities. A young girl named Amy helps her mom at the Fourth of July Butterfly Count. They are searching for a regal fritillaries butterfly, which once "danced over the bluestem grasses, setting the prairie afire with butterfly wings." They count a number of other butterflies before finding regal fritillaries in a very special place on the prairie.

Cone, Molly. *Come Back Salmon: How a Group of Dedicated Kids Adopted Pigeon Creek and Brought It Back to Life.* Photographs by Sidnee Wheelwright. San Francisco, CA: Sierra Club Books for Children, 1992. 0-87156-572-2.

Come Back Salmon tells the story of the students of Jackson Elementary School in Everett, Washington, and how they cleaned up a small creek that flowed past their school. To save the creek, the students had to physically clean large amounts of trash from the stream. They had to present their ideas at local town meetings. They had to raise salmon to release into the stream. They had to keep working to maintain what they started. This book tells a powerful story of what children can do with the right attitude and the support of their teachers.

Domeniconi, David. *M Is for Majestic: A National Parks Alphabet.* Chelsea, MI: Sleeping Bear Press, 2003. 978-1-58536-3339.

This is an alphabet book of the national parks in which each page is illustrated with a painting that captures the scenic highlights of the park. Smaller illustrations in the form of postcards show the reader views of other parks. The companion text briefly describes the national parks and monuments beginning with that same letter. This is a good way for students to learn some of the signature features of the nation's national parks and pick out the places they would most like to visit.

Dunlap, Julie. *Aldo Leopold: Living with the Land.* Illustrated by Antonio Castro. New York: Henry Holt and Company, 1993. 0-8050-2501-4.

Aldo Leopold lived at a time when most people thought the wilderness was for humans to use for themselves. He saw that the land was a delicate balance of interrelationships and that if humans exploit one part, they cause problems in another. His writings and work as a teacher shaped the thoughts of many others. His book *A Sand County Almanac* was very influential both in the way it celebrated the natural world on his farm and in the way he explained the importance of ecology. This straightforward biography tells an important story of an important environmental hero. The book is part of the Earth Keepers series that includes biographies of a number of famous and less-well-known environmental activists.

Dunlap, Julie. *Eye on the Wild: A Story about Ansel Adams.* Illustrated by Kerry Maguire. Minneapolis, MN: Carolrhoda Books, 1995. 0-87614-944-1.

Ansel Adams was both a photographer and environmental activist who used his art to bring awareness and protection to wilderness in the United States. The book begins with Ansel's unconventional childhood and shows how he learned his craft. His summers in the Sierras inspired him to use his photographs to make a difference

Ehrlich, Amy. *Rachel: The Story of Rachel Carson.* Illustrated by Wendell Minor. San
Diego: Silver Whistle, 2003. 0-15-216227-5.

Rachel Carson was a writer and scientist whose books woke people up to the dangers of pesticides and
led to a ban on the use of DDT. Her work helped to bring environmental issues to the forefront and motivated others to become involved. Beginning with her childhood, this book focuses on the significant
events in her life that led to her work as a writer and scientist. Another important aspect of Rachel
Carson's story is the fact that women as scientists were not taken very seriously; she had to be even more
determined to have her voice heard. The text and illustrations show students how she made this happen.

Gartner, Robert. *Careers Inside the World of Environmental Science.* New York: Rosen
Publishing Group, 1995. 0-8239-1903-X.

The book begins with a general introduction to environmental careers and the questions students
should ask themselves if they are considering such a career path. The book includes a wide variety
of careers. There is also information on how to gain experience and find a job. Students can use this
book to help research their environmental careers.

Gazlay, Suzy. *David Suzuki: Doing Battle with Climate Change.* New York: Crabtree Publishing Company, 2009. 978-0-7787-4678-2.

This biography is part of the Voices for Green Choices series that highlights several lesser-known
but important environmental heroes. David Suzuki is a scientist, professor, environmental educator,
and activist. Through these many roles, he has worked to educate people about climate change and
other environmental issues. The book also covers his challenging childhood in Canada and when he
and his family were sent to a Japanese internment camp. The book is filled with photographs and side
notes that include quotes from David Suzuki and information on the issues he is working on.

Grant, Lesley. *Great Careers for People Concerned about the Environment.* Detroit, MI:
Gale Research, 1993. 0-8103-9388-3.

This book features 10 different careers that work to protect the environment, ranging from an environmental lawyer to an environmental chemist. Each profile uses a real person to explain the career.
There are also ideas for how to get started on each career path and activities to try in order to have a
better idea of what each career actually entails.

Harper, Charise Mericle. *Just Grace Goes Green.* Boston, MA: Houghton Mifflin Books,
2009. 978-0-618-95957-0.

This is the story of how Grace's teacher Miss Lois is having the class go green and how Grace
is ready for the challenge. Grace takes on a number of actions to help protect the earth. There are lots
of ideas for class projects, all told in a humorous manner. The superheroes of conservation, imagina-
tive creations that deal with environmental issues are great fun for students to do on their own. Other
activities are practical and can be done by most students.

Herzog, Brad. *S Is for Save the Planet: A How-to-Be Green Alphabet.* Illustrated by Linda
Holt Ayriss. Chelsea, MI: Sleeping Bear Press, 2009. 978-1-58536-482-2.

Brad Herzog has written an alphabet book that can be used with older students as well as young
ones. Each letter is given a page with ideas for solving environmental issues. The focus is on actions
to take, not the problems we have. The sidebars provide background information that will be useful
to parents and older children. The large illustrations make this book visually dramatic.

Hurd, Edith Thatcher, and Clement Hurd. *Wilson's World.* New York: HarperCollins, 1971.
0-06-443359-5.

Wilson is a young boy who loves to paint and tell stories. He paints his own world, and the story it tells
mirrors the changes the world has gone through as it has become more and more crowded. Wilson

realizes he has the power to change things in his work and paints a new beginning for his world. This book is a great way to begin a discussion on what we would do differently if we had a chance to start over.

Jankeliowitch, Anne. *50 Ways to Save the Earth.* Photographs by Philippe Bourseiller. New York: Abrams Books for Young Readers, 2007. 978-0-8109-7239-1.

This attention-grabbing book is beautifully illustrated with photographs of wildlife, people, and stunning places. The photographs set the tone for each of the book's ideas for saving Earth. The topics covered in the book range from solid-waste disposal, endangered species, energy conservation, pollution, and overconsumption. The presentation will grab students' attention, and the background information and ideas are understandable and achievable. The activities give an opening to a class discussion on how to implement some of the ideas.

Lasky, Kathryn. *John Muir: America's First Environmentalist.* Illustrated by Stan Fellows. Cambridge, MA: Candlewick Press, 2006. 978-0-7636-3884-9.

John Muir was one of the most important environmentalists. This picture book biography by Kathryn Lasky takes the reader from John Muir's childhood in Scotland through his journeys in the United States. Students will learn of the significant events that shaped John Muir's life. The book ends with an account of the impact he had on preserving wild areas in the United States. After learning about his life, students can find out more about the impact he had on the beginning of the environmental movement by combining this book with the other biographies of John Muir.

Leuzzi, Linda. *To the Young Environmentalist: Lives Dedicated to Preserving the Natural World.* New York: Franklin Watts, 1997. 0-531-15895-0.

The book is a collection of eight biographies of men and women who worked to help protect the environment in a variety of ways. The book uses photographs, quotes, and text to tell the story of each of environmentalists as they go about their work. Students will learn various ways to make a difference. The book begins with a history of the environmental movement and ends with some new ideas that are making a difference.

Lewis, Barbara. *The Kid's Guide to Social Action: How to Solve the Social Problems You Choose and Turn Creative Thinking into Positive Action.* Edited by Pamela Espeland and Caryn Pernu. Minneapolis, MN: Free Spirit Publishing, 2008.

This book is filled with ideas for students who want to take action to change things in the world. There are suggestions for techniques to write letters, work with the press, use the Internet, change legislation, and more. There are also stories of other young people and the work they have done. This is a very practical guide that will help guide students in taking action. Barbara Lewis has also written a book for teenagers called *The Teen Guide to Social Action* (Minneapolis, MN: Free Spirit Publishing, 1998). Free Spirit Publishing has number of books for students interested in social action.

Locker, Thomas. *John Muir.* Golden, CO: Fulcrum Publishing, 2003. 1-55591-393-8.

John Muir's writing and activism helped to preserve Yosemite National Park and other amazing places across the West. As with all his books, Thomas Locker's illustrations tell a story in themselves as they capture the scenery that inspired John Muir. Quotes from John Muir help this picture book tell the story of this important environmental hero.

Locker, Thomas. *Walking with Henry: Based on the Life and Work of Henry David Thoreau.* Golden, CO: Fulcrum Publishing, 2002. 1555913555.

In this picture book biography, the reader joins Henry David Thoreau on a fictionalized walk in the woods. The students will have a good introduction into Thoreau's ideas about nature and simplicity. His ideas not only sparked a change in the way we think about the natural world, but also influenced Dr. Martin Luther King and many others. As in all his books, Thomas Locker's paintings are stunning.

Magner, Tim. *An Environmental Guide from A to Z*. Illustrated by Aubri Vincent-Barwood. Chicago: Green Sugar Press, 2009. 978-0-9820417-6-5.

This alphabet book is aimed at older elementary students. The in-depth information can easily be used in middle school as well. The illustrations are colorful and lively. Each letter is given a page with plenty of material. There are passages that will be make many aware of some of less-well-known issues and people involved in protecting the environment.

Malnor, Bruce. *Champions of the Wilderness*. Carol Malnor. Illustrations by Anisa Claire Hovemann. Nevada City, CA: Dawn Publications, 2009. 978-1-58469-116-7.

This is a collection of biographies on environmental heroes that focuses on those who have fought to preserve wilderness. This book tells the story of people not covered in other books. Each biography covers the childhood, work, and legacy of the environmental hero. There is an introduction that defines both hero and wilderness. The conclusion has suggestions for ways to become a hero so that the ripples of influence spread the power of our actions.

Maze, Stephanie. *I Want to Be an Environmentalist*. New York: Harcourt, 2000. 0-15-201862-X.

This book highlights a number of ways in which students can have careers helping the environment. There is information on careers such as teaching, wildlife rehabilitators, atmospheric scientists, and others. There is also background information on environmental issues and the history of the environmental movement. There are ideas for actions students can take on their own. The photographs add a lot.

MY Space community with Jeca Taudte. *My Space/Our Planet: Change Is Possible*. New York: HarperCollins, 2008. 978-0-06-156204-4

This book is full of ideas and actions based on ideas from other young people. This book also has suggestions for how to help based on the level of commitment, from simple actions to more complex. The ideas cover many aspects of a young person's life, from clothing, music, games, sports, and more.

Nivola, Claire A. *Planting the Trees of Kenya: The Story of Wangari Maathi*. New York: Farrar, Straus, and Giroux, 2008. 0374399182.

This is the story of Wangari Maathi, an environmentalist and human-rights activist who won the Nobel Peace Prize in 2004. She began the Green Belt Movement, which plants trees and takes on other environmental actions. The book tells her story in a simple, straightforward manner. Along with the watercolor illustrations, the book shows the reader the beauty of Kenya's countryside and the connections Wagari Maathi has with the land. Students will be inspired by the images of trees being planted and the community restored.

Rand, Gloria. *Fighting For the Forest*. Illustrated by Ted Rand. New York: Henry Holt and Company, 1999. 0-8050-5466-9.

This is the story of an old-growth forest in the northwest in which a father and son take regular walks through the trees. One day, they see that the trees have been marked for a clearcut. Their attempt to stop the logging is unsuccessful. The illustration of the pair looking at the tree stumps is very powerful. What makes this such a meaningful story is that even though they are unable to save the forest, they learn what to do the next time.

Riddle, Tohby. *The Singing Hat*. New York: Farrar, Straus, and Giroux, 2001. 0374369348.

Businessman Colin Jenkins sits under a tree and wakes up to find that a bird has made a nest on his head. With his daughter's support, he decides to go about his daily life without disturbing the bird. This proves to be difficult. He ends up losing his job and encounters other challenges. In the end, the baby birds fly away safe and sound. The language of the book is clever and unique as are illustrations that combine a variety of media. This is a great book to discuss the sacrifices one must make when one strongly believes in taking action.

Rodriguez, Rachel. *Building on Nature: The Life of Antoni Gaudi.* Illustrated by Julie Paschkis. New York: Henry Holt and Company, 2009 10:0-8050-8745-1.

Antoni Gaudi was an architect in Spain in the late 1800s and early 1900s. His buildings took inspiration from the natural world. He made an underground chapel from ideas he had from a bat colony. Pillars were made in the shape of animal feet. There were hallways in designs from underwater caverns. The illustrations in this picture book capture the wonder and creativity of Gaudi's buildings. Gaudi was not trying to be an environmentalist, but his work is an example of how we can get ideas by paying attention to the natural world. By celebrating, people increase their awareness of the world around them.

Rose, Deborah Lee. *The People Who Hugged Trees.* Illustrated by Birgitta Saflund. Niwot, CA: Robert Rinehart, 1990.

A folktale set in India 300 years ago tells the story of Amrita Devi, who stands up to the Maharajah when he comes to cut down the trees in her village. He refuses to listen until a terrible windstorm blows through the area. He can see for himself how the trees protected the village and the surrounding lands, so he stops the cuttings. This is a wonderful book to read alongside *Aani and the Tree Huggers.*

Ross, Michael, Elsohn. *Fish Watching, with Eugenie Clark.* Illustrations by Wendy Smith. Minneapolis, MN: Carolrhoda Books, 2000. 1-57505-384-5.

Eugenie Clark fell in love with fish at young age and with that passion became a scientist at a time when few women took that career path. Her research helped people to understand and appreciate sharks and other amazing fish. The book does a good job of showing the challenges as she works toward her accomplishments. Another aspect that makes this a good book for students are the activities they can do that will help them to become fish scientists as well. This book is part of the Naturalist's Apprentice series that includes biographies of several men and women who studied various aspects of the natural world. Each one includes activities so that students can learn about the scientists by doing something hands-on.

Seo, Danny. *Be the Difference, A Beginner's Guide to Changing the World.* Gabriola Island, BC: New Society Publishers. 2001. 0-86571-430-0.

Danny Seo has written a great guide to use with students to help them plan and implement projects that help solve environmental problems. This book is written based on the author's own experience. At the age of 12, he started an environmental-protection organization that grew into a group of 25,000 teenagers. The book includes information on fund-raising, how the government works, working with big businesses, and other practical skills that can help students make a real impact. This book also includes ideas on event planning, media public relations, and how to gain experience. The ideas can support projects both large and small.

Stanley, Phyllis M. *American Environmental Heroes.* Berkeley Heights, NJ: Enslow Publishers, Inc. 1996. 0-89490-630-5.

This is a collection of biographies focused on environmental heroes. Each one is about 10 pages long. The subjects range from well-known figures such as Henry David Thoreau and John Muir, to those who are less well-known, such as David Brower and Ellen Swallow Richards. David Brower was a mountaineer and environmental activist, and Ellen Swallow was the first female scientist at MIT and was instrumental in creating the first drinking-water standards.

Turner, Pamela S. *A Life in the Wild: George Schaller's Struggle to Save the Last Great Beasts.* New York: Melanie Kroupa Books, 2008. 978-0-374-34578-5.

George Schaller is a scientist, writer, photographer, environmental activist, and explorer. He has helped to protect more than 190,000 square miles of wilderness, and his efforts have led to the protection of wide variety of endangered species. This biography focuses on a different part of the world where George Schaller worked. The book is illustrated with his photographs. Even if students do not read the entire book and just read a chapter or two, they will be inspired by the work of this multitalented man and his adventures around the world.

Wellington, Monica. *Riki's Birdhouse*. New York: Dutton Children's Books, 2009. 978-0-525-42079-8.

To attract bluebirds to his backyard, Riki builds a birdhouse. This book shows each step he takes in making the birdhouse and all the other things he does to attract birds to his yard. It all works wonderfully and Riki has a backyard filled with birds. Journal entries in the illustrations tell the reader more about what Riki is observing. On the last page, there are illustrations of common backyard birds and a challenge to match them up with birds drawn on other pages of the book.

Yarrow, Joanna. *How to Reduce Your Carbon Footprint: 365 Simple Ways to Save Energy, Resources, and Money*. San Francisco: Chronicle Books, 2008. 978-0-8118-6393-3.

Joanna Yarrow has written a simple resource of ideas for students who want to take action in their lives and to educate others. The topics covered focus on lowering our carbon footprint through changes in personal lifestyles. There are lots of sidebars with quick facts and statistics that summarize the issues.

Activities

This last chapter has activities that will provide students with the skills and knowledge to help them solve the environmental issues facing our world. The objective of these activities is to help students gain the skills and knowledge they need in order to make changes and take action. Most of these activities are not meant to deal with any one particular issue. They can be adapted and used with a variety of the environmental issues discussed in this book. To be effective, students will need information. By using library resources, they will become knowledgeable about the issues and learn the skills they will need to become lifelong learners regarding environmental issues.

Environmental Foundation

One way people help the environment is to make financial contributions to organizations that work to protect the environment. However, when people donate money, they want to be sure it is being put to good use and will not be wasted.

Materials: research materials

Procedure:
The students will study various environmental organizations and select one or more to be the recipient of a financial contribution. There are a two ways you can start this activity: one is to use money that the students have raised or tell them they have an imaginary $1,000 and ask them to decide which organization will receive it. This is a good way for students to learn how environmental groups work. It is also a good opportunity for students to use critical-thinking skills to decide which of the many worthwhile environmental organizations they would like to support.

Put the students in small groups to discuss the issues they care about the most. Have them brainstorm questions they should ask and answer in evaluating a charity. For example:

What are the characteristics of a good charity?

How is the charity working to solve problems?

How large is the charity?

How long has the charity been in existence?

How much of the donation will go directly to working on the issues?

Next, each student picks one charity to investigate that is working on the issues of concern. After doing some research, the groups of students share the information and as a class reach a consensus about which organization to support. The students will have to be both good listeners and speakers to reach an agreement.

Besides going to individual Web sites for each organization, a good source to use for research is the Charity Navigator at http://www.charitynavigator.org/. It provides information on many charities, their finances, and their effectiveness.

Even if the students do not have any actual money to donate, this activity may very well inspire them to raise money to donate to a worthy cause.

Environmental Career Day

There are more and more career possibilities in environmental fields. In fact, many careers that your students will choose as adults do not even exist yet. Learning more about these options can help to inspire your students to realize there are many ways to make a difference.

Materials: research materials

Procedure:
Students will learn about the various environmental careers and share what they have learned. This is a list of some of the career possibilities:

Wildlife biologist
Environmental lawyer
Environmental activist
Wastewater plant manager
Zoo curator
Environmental educator
Outdoor trip leader
Scientist (biologist, zoologist, herpetologist, etc.)
Environmental engineer
Urban planner/architect
Forest ranger
Fund-raiser for an environmental organization
Researcher for an environmental organization
Ecotourism guide
Game warden
Solar design engineer
Waste-management specialist

There are many more possibilities beyond this list. In fact, many traditional careers now have environmental-protection aspects.

The students should select a career and answer the following questions:

What does a _____ do?
How does this work help the environment?
What kind of training does one need for this career?
What are the challenges in this career?
What other interesting information can you find?

Students should use the research materials to find information and make contact with someone who is working in the field. This way they will have a primary source of information.

Once the students have gathered the information, they have an opportunity to share what they have learned. They can create a booth where they can teach others about the careers they have studied. They can make posters, create resumes, hold interviews, and have a job fair, or simply present to the class to share their knowledge about the careers.

Students should understand that there are many ways to make a difference in the world. The key is to find a way to use one's interests, skills, and passion in a career that will put it all to good use while making a difference.

The Vocational Information Center's Web site has links to various resources for career exploration at http://www.khake.com/page46.html.

Wisconsin's Division of Natural Resources Environmental Education for Kids has very helpful information at http://www.dnr.wi.gov/eek/job/index.htm.

Improving Wildlife Habitats

There are major benefits to improving wildlife habitats around the schoolyard, home, and neighborhood. One benefit is to the animals; both large and small will have more places to live. The other advantage is to people; a healthier wildlife habitat is also a healthier human habitat. In addition, people of all ages gain a great deal from the experience of seeing more wildlife. These experiences strengthen the connections needed to create support for environmental protection.

Materials: varies depending on the project

Procedure:

Depending on your site, there are many ways both large and small that you and your students can improve the wildlife habitat around your school.

Wildlife Habitat Improvement Ideas

1. Grow more native plants that provide food and shelter for a variety of wildlife. The key is to grow native plants since they require the least care and provide the greatest amount of food and shelter for native animals.

2. Put out a birdbath or some other source of water.

3. Set up bird feeders designed for native birds, not starlings or house sparrows. These non-native birds are aggressive and have led to a decline in native songbirds.

4. Cover holes and openings in and around schools, houses, and buildings where house sparrows and starlings may nest.

5. Encourage people to keep their cats indoors or put a bell on the cat if it is going to go outdoors. Cats kill millions of songbirds each year.

6. Work together with your neighbors and other schools to create a larger area of improved wildlife habitat.

7. Besides food and water wildlife needs shelter. Create shelters by building bird houses, bat houses, or butterfly houses. Certain plantings can also improve natural shelters or just put out sticks for a brush pile.

8. Grow an organic lawn. A lawn without pesticides and herbicides will attract more wildlife and create a healthier habitat.

9. Create a simple nature spot by letting plants grow wild in a section of the schoolyard. Just stop mowing and see what happens. Remember, insects and other invertebrates are wildlife as well.

10. Laying out some old boards and logs creates habitats for salamanders and a wide variety of invertebrates.

More information can be obtained from a local nursery or garden store. A good Web site to use for support is the National Wildlife Federation, which provides ideas and information to design a backyard and schoolyard habitat. They also have a program to certify a backyard or schoolyard as wildlife habitat at http://www.nwf.org/gardenforwildlife/.

Extensions:

Once the students have information for creating wildlife habitat in their community, they can design the ideal backyard or schoolyard. They can create a map of a backyard designed for wildlife. On a piece of graph paper, students draw a map to scale that includes places for food, water, and shelter. The plan should be as specific as possible, including the plant species, costs, and names of animals that will be attracted to the backyard and other fun features, including ones for humans.

Invent a Solution

Technology will not solve every environmental problem, and it would be a mistake to think we can just keep doing what we are doing and hope for some technological miracle that will solve everything. However, there have been new inventions that have helped to ease environmental problems. These ideas are born of creative thinking.

Other ideas can be developed from understanding biomimicry. Biomimicry is a term used to describe the idea that nature should be a model for how humans do things in order to live with the earth instead of against the earth. Biomimicry is a new science that studies nature's models and then imitates or takes inspiration from these designs to find a better way for humans to do things. Nature has had almost 4 billion years to get things right and create a system that works. There is a lot we can learn from how nature operates. Instead of viewing what we can get from the natural world, we should look for what we can learn.

In her book *Biomimicry: Innovation Inspired by Nature*, Janine M. Benyus explains several principles we can learn from the natural world that can help us to conduct business in an environmentally sustainable manner.

1. Use waste as a resource: Decaying leaves become part of the soil and help the trees grow. Are there ways our waste can be used to make something else?

2. Diversify and cooperate: Living organisms work together in symbiotic relationships that help both survive. Are there ways people can work together to improve the way we build things?

3. Gather and use energy efficiently: Leaves turn to get the most sunlight. What can we do to use energy more efficiently?

4. Optimize rather than maximize: Bigger is not always better, efficiency is what counts. Animals do not build homes bigger than they need to be.

5. Use materials sparingly: Bird bones are hollow but very strong. How can we use fewer materials but still make quality products?

6. Don't foul their nests: Organisms do not create anything that will poison them and leave it where they live. Birds clean out their nests by carrying away the droppings. Snakes do not make any more poison than they need at a time. How can we be sure to keep our home truly clean?

7. Don't draw down the resources: Herd animals move around so that they do not eat all the grasses in one place. How can we avoid using non-renewable resources faster than we can develop substitutes for them, and how do we avoid using renewable resources before they have a chance to grow back?

8. Remain in balance with the biosphere: The key elements of life move in cycles through the biosphere. How do we create cycles so the same materials are used again and again?

9. Shop locally: Animals get everything they need right in their own habitat. How do we get more of we need from our own communities to avoid the cost in resource to transport materials from far away?

The students select a product or process that they want to redesign to make it more environmentally sustainable. To understand how to solve a problem, one must know its effects and the reason there is a problem in the first place. If they are working on redesigning a process such as how food is served in a restaurant, they can visit the place and learn firsthand about the way things are done. To begin to redesign a product, they should learn about the product's life cycle. The students can go to one of the following Web sites to learn how an everyday product is made and the environmental impact in making it or to pick their own product and do the necessary research.

Useful Web sites:

These articles from *Sierra Magazine* from the Sierra Club are on the hidden life of various products: http://search.atomz.com/search/?sp-q=Hidden+Life&sp-t=sierra_magazine&sp-a=sp1001da90&sp-q-1= Sierra&sp-x-1=collection.

Sanford University's Alliance for Manufacturing has a Web site with short videos explaining how various products are made at http://manufacturing.stanford.edu/.

The Worldwatch Institute has a Web page entitled "Good Stuff? A Behind-the-Scenes Guide to the Things We Buy" that will also help students with their research at http://www.worldwatch.org/taxonomy/term/44.

Copying Nature

Using their own creativity and ideas from biomimicry, students can invent new products and processes that have less impact on the environment.

Materials: craft supplies, paper, drawing materials

Procedure:
Students should reflect on all the environmental issues they have learned about and pick one that concerns them the most. Thinking about the causes of the problem, the students will create a new invention that will help solve it. They can either draw their ideas or make a 3-D model.

National Parks

One of the United States' greatest ideas was the creation of the national park system, beginning with Yellowstone National Park in 1872. The idea for national parks was to preserve places in the United States with unique scenic features and habitats for plants and animals. Millions of people visit the parks for recreation, education, and the opportunity to witness the wonders of these special places. Across the United States, there are many places where land is protected to preserve the habitat, protect its beauty, and give people the opportunity to enjoy the outdoors.

Materials: research tools

Procedure:
Students create a brochure or travel guide to a national park of their choice. The same activity can be done using a state park, county park, or local nature preserve. If possible allow them to use any personal experiences they have had at a national park or other preserve. The travel guide to the park should include the following:
　　When was the park created?
　　What special features does the park have to offer?
　　Where is the park located?
　　What do you need to know if you are planning a visit?
　　What did the creation of the park protect?
　　Include other interesting facts.
　　The brochure should include some photographs or images from the park. This project can also be done in a simpler fashion by having the students simply write a letter to their families describing their imaginary trip.

The Web site for the National Park Service is http://www.nps.gov/index.htm.

Another source of information for older students is the documentary by Ken Burns entitled *The National Parks, America's Best Idea* at http://www.pbs.org/nationalparks/.

Environmental Pen Pals

To learn about what is happening in the environment in other places, students can have a pen pal they can contact to find out about environmental issues around the country and around the world.

Materials: letter-writing materials

Procedure:

If you do not have your own connections with a teacher in another place, ask around the school for suggestions. After making an introduction, students can ask questions, such as what is the environment like where you live? What kind of problems are you facing in your community? What kind of plants and animals live near your home?

Environmental Club

Students can make a difference. There are many examples of changes that have been made by young people. There are many different ways for students to take action in their schools by educating, motivating, and changing things. This can begin by helping students start their own school environmental club.

Materials: varies with project

Procedure:

There are many ways to organize the club depending on your situation. This may be an after-school project or an in-school class project. You can help students get started by acting as a guide; get them to think about themselves and their lives. The first question students should ask themselves is, what issue concerns me the most? The next two questions are: What do I love to do? What am I good at? The best ideas for projects take a student's passions and skills and put them to good use.

By being creative, any passion and skill can make a difference. Students should focus on a simple, reasonable, practical project. If a student loves writing, his or her project should require writing; for example, writing a book to educate others or a letter to a government official. A student who loves drawing can design posters that are hung up in area restaurants. A student adept at computers can create a PowerPoint presentation, movie, or games. A student with a flair for the dramatic can perform a skit for younger students. Whatever the skill, there is a project that can be done. Here are some project ideas.

1. Recycling: Many organizations collect items to be recycled. Students can organize a drive to collect items to be recycled or reused.

   Cell phones: http://www.grcrecycling.com/

   Batteries: http://www.batteryrecycling.com/

   Shoes: http://www.soles4souls.org/

   Juice boxes: http://www.terracycle.net/

2. Education: There are a number of projects the students can do to educate other people about environmental issues. The students can:

   Create a PowerPoint presentation

   Produce a movie

   Perform a skit

Make a speech

Teach a lesson

Make public-service announcements

Lead nature walks on the school grounds

Build a nature trail

Hold an environmental fair

Create environmental bumper stickers

3. Hold a fund-raiser to support an environmental organization.

4. Work with the administration to make the school more environmentally sustainable. Possible projects include:

Paper recycling

No-idling policy

Energy conservation

Pesticides ban

5. Write a book.

6. Have a contest for the best essay, poster, bumper sticker, logo, or some other project.

To make this work, you will have to adjust your involvement to meet the students' needs; some will need more guidance than others. There is a true sense of pride when students complete a project and have done more than just learned about a problem. Even a small accomplishment is better than no accomplishment. The value in not just in the product but also in the process that they go through to get there. What they learn in this process will serve them well in the future.

Real Research

Materials: varies with projects

Procedure:
Helping to solve environmental problems means understanding the science behind the issues. Through environmental monitoring, students can help scientists gather the information they need to help protect the environment. On the national, state, and local levels, organizations are conducting research to monitor changes in the environment. They count on citizens to help in this effort by going out into the field to collect information.

Here are some projects that you may want to become involved in. In addition, check with your state's environmental department and environmental organizations for other local opportunities.

Journey North has monitoring projects on animal migration, plants, and seasonal changes at http://www.learner.org/jnorth/.

The Cornell Laboratory of Ornithology has a number of monitoring projects related to counting birds at http://www.birds.cornell.edu/pfw/.

The World Wide Biome Project is a monitoring project studying your local biome and sharing the information with others around the world at http://www2.kpr.edu.on.ca/cdciw/biomes/.

The National Wildlife Federation has a monitoring program called Wildlife Watch, a nationwide nature-watching program, at http://www.nwf.org/wildlifewatch/.

Students can also begin their own environmental monitoring project on the school grounds. Start simple by focusing on one aspect of the local environment. The key is to observe and record information over time. As you add new information each year, the classes are creating a database that can be used to monitor the local environment and track changes that may signal an improvement or a drop in the health of the environment.

Monitoring project ideas:

• Record the arrival of migrating birds in the spring.

• Record the amount of snow each winter.

• Track when local wildflowers bloom.

• Track when the leaves fall off trees in the schoolyard.

• Estimate the population of squirrels or some other animal.

• Each year, sample the number of invertebrates in a square meter of lawn, in a stream, in a pond, or in another nearby habitat.

• Measure the growth of lichen on trees.

Gardens

One way to save energy and resources is to eat more locally grown, organic foods. When the food is grown close to where it is being sold, there are less energy costs for transportation. When the food is grown organically without pesticides and chemical fertilizers, there are fewer environmental impacts as well. To teach students the ideas behind organic, locally grown food, the garden does not have to be a large undertaking. Many vegetables can be grown in pots indoors or you can select vegetables for an outdoor garden that grow quickly in the spring before school lets out.

Here are some types of vegetables that can be grown in containers: cucumbers, pole green beans, leaf lettuce, peppers, radishes, squash, and tomatoes. You should select varieties that do not grow to a large size. The vegetables grow best in containers with enough drainage to keep the soil from becoming saturated. Clay pots work the best but even a bucket with holes can work. The most fertile soil is a mix of compost, peat moss, and dirt. Leafy vegetables tend to need less sun than vegetables such as tomatoes and peppers, which need more. Earth boxes are simple, prepackaged container gardens that can be used in a school setting to grow vegetables. Find more information at http://www.earthbox.com/.

Even if the students only grow enough vegetables for one or two salads, they are still learning important concepts about our agricultural system and being a part of a food cycle.

As an extension, the students can make a meal of food produced within 50 miles of their homes or have a taste-test comparing organic foods with non-organic foods.

Be a City Planner

Materials: art supplies, assorted recycled and reused items

Procedure:
Students will either draw or create a model of a green city. The level of expectation will vary depending on the age of your students and their background knowledge. Here are some points the students should consider when designing their towns:

How can we increase the amount of open space in the town?

How do we lessen the dependence on cars in the town?

What kinds of businesses should we have in the town?

What laws and regulations should we have to improve the environment in the town?

How can buildings be built to improve the environment?

What can we do to preserve habitats for plants and animals?

What can we do to have less waste?

Current Events

Understanding and becoming aware of the environmental issues in your community is a key to understanding and becoming aware of environmental issues in other places. It is these local issues where students can best use their skills and energy to make a difference.

Check your local newspaper on a regular basis to keep up-to-date on environmental issues in the community. Local environmental groups will have information as well. Be on the lookout for articles on air or water pollution, new housing and business developments, new legislation, traffic, and other topics. Keep up-to-date yourself on the issues and learn what students can do about them.

Read articles with students to help them understand the background and other issues related to the topic. Be sure that they understand the who, what, where, when, and why of the issues you are discussing.

Depending on the community, there may be more then one topic to discuss, or the whole class can focus on one issue.

Reaction Responses

Materials: newspaper articles on environmental issues

Procedure:
The students read an article on an environmental issue and first summarize the article in a short paragraph. Next, they write a response to the article answering one or more of these prompts:
    What is your reaction to the issue?
    How would you resolve the conflict?
    What do you think will happen next?
    What questions do you have?
    Extension: Create a newscast of local environmental issues.

Community Meetings

Materials: depends on the project

Procedure:
Another way to use the current events in your community is as the basis of a role-playing activity. The event can be the subject of a community meeting. If there is not an issue that works with this activity, you can create a simulation so that students can gain the experience by role-playing a town meeting. Use as much local information as possible to make the simulation as realistic as possible.

Begin by explaining to the children that government officials hold community meetings to gather input from concerned citizens to help them make decisions regarding local issues in the community. Here is an outline that can be used to get the class started.

The situation:

A proposal has been brought to the community legislature to build a build a small shopping center in an undeveloped area just on the edge of town. The plan calls for 10 stores and a parking lot. Divide the students into the following groups:

The Redfield Business Group: They are the developers of the project.

The Redfield Environmental Group: They are a local environmental group.

The Redfield Parents Association: They are the local child advocate organization.

The Redfield Chamber of Commerce: They are the local business association.

Town legislators: These are the students who will decide if the Redfield Business Group's project will be approved.

The students in each group will take on the point of view of the group to which they have been assigned. While there is room to be creative as the students state their cases, they also need to be respectful to the other groups and be realistic in their statements and actions. Depending on the age of the students, you may have to be more involved in helping them organize their presentations and questions.

The meeting will have six parts.

Part one: The Redfield Business Group (developers of the project) will come up with the details of the project. They should be able to explain why this is a good idea and how it will benefit the community through tax money, jobs, and other improvements. The students can add more details to what they are proposing and other aspects of the plan that will help them convince the town legislators to approve their permit to build.

The Redfield Business group will make its proposal while legislators and interested citizen groups listen to the plan.

Part two: After giving the advocacy groups time to plan questions, each group has the opportunity to ask their questions to the developers.

Part three: The groups ask their questions. Depending on your students' abilities, there are two ways to proceed at this point. Either have each group ask their questions all at once and then sit with the business group to help them craft answers to the questions, or another option is to simply have the business group answer the questions as they are asked with less assistance from you.

Part four: This is more of an open forum where each group can ask questions and make comments.

Part five: The county legislators have been listening but now they have the opportunity to ask any remaining questions. Then they go to their "offices" to reach their decision.

Part six: After having reached a conclusion, the legislators announce their decision.

The parts will have to be done over time to give you a chance to meet with each group to explain their role and get them started on preparing for the community meeting.

Speaking Up and Out

Effecting positive change in our environment means understanding how local, state, and national governments work. When students are taught how our elected officials make laws and render decisions, they are also learning how to help the environment. Some of the current events the students read about will be about new legislation and other issues that involve government decision-making. This can be an opportunity for students to become involved in the process. Now that students are more aware of environmental issues, they will see plenty of examples of them in their daily lives. They should realize they have the power and ability to speak up.

The first step for students is to research the issue in order to become experts. They need to able to do more than just complain. Speaking with elected officials is also the time to offer suggestions and solutions. Students can contact elected officials through letters, phone calls, petitions, e-mails, and town meetings. Arrangements can be made to visit government offices or invite officials to speak to the class.

Students should know the names of their congressperson, senator, state representative, mayor, and any other elected official and how to get in touch with them

Survey Web sites for the elected officials to find out what they are doing to protect the environment. If there is something going on in the school that they would like to see changed, they can speak up and try to change it. However, it is not enough to just complain; they will also have to provide a possible solution.

Local Heroes

Children need heroes and it is important for them to realize there are heroes in their own community. They will do this by researching and telling the story of a local environmental organization. The goal of this project is to provide students with models that will inspire them to help themselves and others to protect the environment. By learning about people and events in their community, children will hopefully feel a closer connection to where they live. They will learn that good work is being done and that there is hope.

Materials: research materials

Procedure:

Step one: Provide students with as many of the biographies listed in the beginning of the chapter as you can. The students can read the books in groups or on their own. After reading each book, they answer the following questions:

Who did you read about?

What did they do to help the environment?

Was there something in their childhood that inspired them to become an environmentalist?

What challenges did they have to overcome to accomplish their goals?

What techniques did the author use to tell the hero's story in an interesting way?

What is left to do?

Step two: In every community, there are organizations working on improving the local environment. They range from national and regional organizations such as the Sierra Club and Audubon Society, which have local chapters in most parts of the country, to countless local groups working in every community to help make a difference.

To find organizations and individuals to celebrate, ask around or use the phone book, Internet, local library, or government offices. Local nature centers are another possibility for the subject of the biography.

Step three: Once you have a list of possible organizations, it is time for students to work together in small groups to shine a light on the good work that is being done. This project can be done on an individual basis or as a group project. Students will need to find the following information as well as anything else they deem interesting. The worksheet can be used for students to record their notes.

Name of organization. _____
_____

What does the organization do to help the environment? _____
_____

What are the issues involved in the problems you are trying to solve? _____
_____

How does your organization raise money? _____
_____

What are your organization's proudest achievements? _____
_____

What are your organization's goals? _____
_____

What are some of the challenges? _____
_____

How can people help your group make a difference? _____
_____

What tactics do you use to accomplish your goals? _____
_____

How did people in the organization become interested in this issue? _____
_____

What inspired you to become involved in the organization? _____
_____
_____

Step four: The next step is to answer these questions and any others the students come up with over the course of the project.

The main source of information is to talk directly with the people who work in the organization. While it is possible to talk to someone on the phone or to use e-mail, the most meaningful and efficient way is to talk to someone directly. Practice interviewing skills so that students can get the most out of the experience. There may also be newspaper or magazine articles about the organization that will have information students can use.

One source of information is materials written by the organization in the form of brochures, pamphlets, Web sites, magazines, annual reports, newsletters, and other materials. The students should look at what the group has published to try to answer some of their questions.

It will be important to learn more background information on the issues from various research materials. This will help students understand the work being done.

Once all the information has been gathered, it is time to celebrate the work of the organization. The students can write books or create awards, PowerPoint presentations, videos, or other ways to present the story. The important thing is to find a way to spread the word and reach an audience beyond the school.

The final step is to decide how the class will celebrate the work of each organization. They could write a book, make posters, design a PowerPoint presentation, create an award, make a speech, or find some other means of sharing the good works.

Science Share

Students will design and conduct experiments comparing the qualities of environmental friendly products with more traditional products. In addition, this set of lessons helps students understand the process of science by learning to conduct experiments. The scientific process is the step-by-step method that scientists use to gather facts and observations that lead to accurate and reliable results. It also gives students the opportunity to apply what they learn from their experiments to make thoughtful decisions regarding consumer products. In the end, students can make recommendations regarding which products to buy given the price, the quality, the environmental impact, and other features.

Part One: Model Experiment

Materials: three brands of plastic wrap, if possible make one eco-friendly, marbles, bowls

Procedure:
The first step is to understand how to design an experiment that will yield accurate results. To teach the students this important science skill, conduct the first experiment together as a class comparing three different brands of plastic wrap.

Steps to an Experiment

1. Question: Every experiment begins with a question. The question should be specific, not a general question, such as which plastic wrap works the best? In this case, is not clear what is meant by best. Have the students brainstorm some possible questions for studying plastic wrap. For example:

   Which brand of plastic wrap is stickiest?

   Which brand is strongest?

   Which brand keeps food the freshest?

   Which brand is the hardest to poke a hole through?

   Which brand can be stretched the farthest?

2. Hypothesis: After a question has been chosen, the next step is to record the hypothesis. The hypothesis is the scientist's predicted answer to the question. For example, I predict brand A will be the stickiest because the wrap is thicker.

3. <u>Plan the Procedure:</u> Now it is time to design an experiment that will answer the question. In designing any experiment, one must consider the possible variables. A variable is a factor that can be changed in an experiment.

   Manipulated variable: This is the variable the scientist changes deliberately in order to answer the question.

   Controlled variables: These are the variables that the scientists keep the same so that it is clear what causes the results. A well-designed experiment has only one manipulated variable and all the rest are controlled.

   The procedure should result in information that is expressed as quantitative data. Quantitative data is information that is expressed in numbers. If the procedure is one that is based on a survey technique or opinion, a scale of 1 to 10 can be used to present the results as quantitative data. The directions of the procedure should be written out with exact numbers whenever possible so the experiment can be repeated accurately.

   Model Procedure:

1. Put four marbles in a paper bowl and cover it with a six-inch by six-inch piece of plastic wrap.

2. Wrap the plastic as tight as possible around the bowl.

3. Hold the bowl upside down the same way.

4. Turn the bowl over and time how long it takes for the marbles to fall out. The other controls in this experiment are:

   Use the same bowl.

   Use the same kind of marbles.

5. <u>Recording the results:</u> Scientists do not just rely on their memories to remember the results. In order to be as accurate as possible, the students record their results on a chart as they go through their trials.

6. <u>Test the experiment:</u> Often, our first attempt at conducting an experiment does not work; something in the procedure may make it difficult to get accurate results. This means that the procedure may need a small adjustment or may even need to be completely revised.

7. <u>Conduct the experiment:</u> Students now carefully conduct the experiments, measuring each step. After each trial, they should record the results accurately. To be sure the results are accurate and not one extreme or the other, scientists conduct experiments more than once.

8. <u>Drawing conclusions:</u> Based on the results, the students draw conclusions about which plastic wrap is the stickiest. However, the stickiest brand may not necessarily be the brand that the students recommend. Other factors to consider are the price per unit, the quality, the impact on the environment, packaging, and other things. Taking all this into account, the students make a recommendation of which brand is best to buy.

<u>Part Two</u>

Students should now select their own product to study. Here is a list of consumer products that they can investigate that include an environmentally friendly choice:

   Paper towels

   Laundry soap

   Dish soap

   Glass cleaner

   All-purpose cleaner

   Carpet cleaner

Bathroom cleaner

Diapers

Wipes

Napkins

Tissues

Paper plates

Toilet paper

Paper bowls

Kitchen garbage bags

Glue

Tape

Pens

Crayons

Soap

Baggies

Garbage bags

Tinfoil

Ice melting crystals

Once students have selected a product to study, they will conduct the experiments in school to study the product's quality. These rubrics can be used to evaluate the students' work

Process Rubric

Name:

1—not at all; 2—poor; 3—adequate; 4—good; 5—excellent

___ Design an experiment with at least four controls.

___ Conduct at least three trials carefully.

___ Record results accurately.

___ Stay on task.

___ Cooperate with others.

___ Clean up materials and respect classroom space.

The students can also write lab reports and create displays in order to share the information they have gathered.

Rubric for Lab Reports

Name:

0 points = not done; 1 point = needs improvement; 2 points = good; 3 points = excellent

1. Question
   ___ Clearly state operational question (include the brand names).
2. Hypothesis
   ___ Write your hypothesis and explain your reasoning.
3. Materials
   ___ List all the materials you used.
4. Procedure
   ___ Write every step of your procedure. (Be sure to include amounts used.)
5. Summary (Be sure to write this in order.)
   ___ Restate the question.
   ___ Identify your controls and your variable: "My controls in this lab were ..." (at least four).
   ___ Answer your question.
   ___ Defend your answer using quantitative data.
   ___ What qualitative data did you observe?
   ___ What do you think made the winning brand better?
   ___ Explain if your hypothesis was correct or incorrect.
   ___ Given the price, ecological impact, and quality, which product would you recommend and why?
   ___ Explain at least two ways your experiment could have been improved.
   ___ Describe any other questions that have developed from your experiment (at least two).
6. Writing style
   ___ Grammar (verb tense, punctuation, paragraphs, etc.)
   ___ Spelling (use spell check)
   ___ Style (easy to read, well written, edited)
7. Results
   ___ List your results in an understandable and organized chart and graph.
   ___ Create a graph using only the averages from your results.
   ___ Label and title your chart and graph that explains what you studied.
   ___ Price per unit of product in the chart.

Extensions:
Hold a science share to show parents, teachers, and others the results of the experiments. The students can make displays on posterboards or trifolds to teach people about the products. Here is a rubric that can be used to evaluate the work.

Display Rubric
___ Display board handed in on time
___ Display includes:

graph

chart

product samples

drawing of procedure

lab report

photo of self

___ Creativity

___ Organization

___ Presentation at science share

Alternative Cleaning

There are many cleaners that can be made from non-toxic, household ingredients. Students can make the cleaners and compare them to store-bought equivalents to test how they work.

Materials: varies depending on what cleaner is being made

Procedure:
Students make a homemade cleaning product and test its effectiveness against store-bought cleaners.

Here are some examples of safe alternatives to store-bought cleaners:

Appliance cleaner: 1 tsp borax, 2 tbsp vinegar, 1/4 tsp liquid soap, and 2 cups of water.
Cream soft scrub: 1/2 cup baking soda, vegetable-based juice, and liquid soap. Stir into creamy paste and use as a sponge rinse.
Window cleaner: 1 tsp liquid soap, 3 tbsp vinegar, and 2 cups of water in a spray bottle.
Floor cleaner: 1/2 cup liquid soap, 1/2 cup lemon juice, and 2 gallons of warm water.
Stain removers:
Ink: cold water, 1 tbsp cream of tartar, and 1 tbsp lemon juice.
General spots: club soda or lemon juice.
Bathroom cleaners: Make a paste of borax and lemon juice; leave overnight and wipe in the morning.
Tub and tile cleaner: 1/2 cup of baking soda, 1 cup white vinegar, and warm water.
Rug cleaner: club soda.

Extension:
The students can take a look at the labels of the cleaning supplies in their homes and record what the cleaners are made from as well as any warnings on the container.

References

Benyus, Janine M. *Biomimicry: Innovation Inspired by Nature*. New York: Harper Perennial, 1998. 0-06-053322-6.

The Biomimicry Institute. http://www.biomimicryinstitute.org/.

Index

About the Author

DANIEL A. KRIESBERG's lifetime passion for the environment began as child, when his third-grade teacher assigned him a project on backyard birds. He went on to work as a naturalist, an elementary school teacher, and an environmental-education consultant, and is currently working as a sixth-grade science teacher at Friends Academy in Locust Valley, New York. He has written several books, including *A Sense of Place: Teaching Children about the Environment with Picture Books*, as well as more than 100 magazine articles on environmental-education topics.

Dan lives with his wife, Karen, and sons Zack and Scott in Bayville, New York. As much as possible, he spends time outdoors and tries to lead a green lifestyle, despite the challenges of modern suburban life.